# Carmarthenshire

## 40 favourite Walks

The author and publisher have made every effort to ensure that the information in this publication is accurate, and accept no responsibility whatsoever for any loss, injury or inconvenience experienced by any person or persons whilst using this book.

published by
**pocket mountains ltd**
The Old Church, Annanside,
Moffat DG10 9HR

ISBN: 978-1-907025-80-8

Text and photography copyright © Julian Rollins 2022

The right of Julian Rollins to be identified as the Author of this work has been asserted by him in accordance with the Copyright, Designs and Patents Act 1988

A catalogue record for this book is available from the British Library

Contains Ordnance Survey data © Crown copyright and database 2025

All rights reserved. No part of this publication may be reproduced, stored in a retrieval system, or transmitted in any form or by any means, electronic or mechanical, including photocopying and recording, unless expressly permitted by Pocket Mountains Ltd.

Printed by J Thomson Colour Printers, Glasgow

# Introduction

Carmarthenshire is a big county; of the old counties of Wales, it's the largest. As the crow flies, it's a little more than 70km from Efailwen, on the border with Pembrokeshire, to Halfway, on the Powys border in the Brecon Beacons. It's also a county of contrasts. Along the coast you'll walk close to the airy edges of tall cliffs, but there are beaches too, some so long you can't see an end to them, and sheltered estuaries, like the 'heron priested shore' at Laugharne that inspired the poet Dylan Thomas.

Inland there are tucked-away valleys and castle-topped hills, open moorland and ancient woodland that is fizzing with life. There's plenty to explore.

Most of the routes in this book have been devised to be straightforward and easy to follow. They are also intended to be manageable as a morning or afternoon outing. Many are close to some sort of attraction (perhaps a garden, a castle or just a first-class tearoom), so that the two experiences can be combined.

Every effort has been made to provide a detailed route description that, with the route sketch map, will keep you on track. However, it is recommended that you also take an Ordnance Survey map along when you walk, especially on upland routes. It also makes good sense to check the weather forecast before you set out. Carmarthenshire's climate is mild, but its weather has its moments. It is changeable, especially in spring and autumn, so take along plenty of layers, including something wind and rainproof.

## History

What came first – Carmarthen or Carmarthenshire? Unlike the chicken-egg conundrum, this question is easy to answer because the town of Carmarthen is very, very old.

In fact, it can make a claim to be one of Wales' oldest urban communities. The first written record of what became Carmarthen dates back to the first century AD, when Claudius Ptolemy of Alexandria compiled his gazetteer of the Roman world, *Geography*. Ptolemy noted that the people of what is now Carmarthenshire and Pembrokeshire were the Demetae, and wrote of a town that he called Moridunum. A later itinerary for Roman travellers in Britain gave Carmarthen the name Muridunum.

Both names are thought to be a Latinisation of British elements – *mori* for 'sea' and *dunos* for 'fort'. Their 'sea fort', Carmarthen, was an important outpost at the western edge of Rome's empire.

So, Carmarthen as a town dates back at least 1900 years to Ptolemy's time. The county of Carmarthenshire is a much more recent invention. From the 12th century the area around the royal castle of Carmarthen was effectively a county. But the boundaries of the modern county did not come into being until the 1530s, when King Henry VIII moved to make local administration in Wales more like the set-up in England.

Wherever you go in Carmarthenshire you're rarely that far from a castle. Following the Battle of Hastings it took the Normans a few decades or so to assert control over England, but Wales proved to be more of a challenge. Semi-independent 'marcher' lordships were created by Norman warlords where they could grab some land and build a castle to help keep hold of what had been grabbed. The native princes of Wales responded with castles of their own. So, you'll find Norman fortresses, such as the one at Kidwelly, and Welsh ones, like Dinefwr.

Many, like the stronghold at Newcastle Emlyn (it's only relatively 'new', as it was built in 1240), changed hands a time or two over the centuries.

#### Flora and fauna

The very varied landscapes of Carmarthenshire make for some great nature-watching opportunities. For the most part the coast is gently sloping with a big tidal range, which means there are large areas of marsh and mudflats for foraging shorebirds. This inter-tidal zone is perfect for winter birdwatching. You can see large flocks of wading birds, such as oystercatchers, knot and dunlin.

Head inland for open moorland, fast-flowing rivers and oak-rich woodland, which flush with bluebells every spring. The upland woods of Carmarthenshire, such as the RSPB's Gwenffrwd-Dinas nature reserve, ring with birdsong in spring and summer.

Lastly, just about everywhere you go, there's a good chance that you will see a high-flying red kite. The distinctive raptor's sparing use of slow, steady wingbeats can keep it in the air for hours at a time. The species came close to extinction in Britain in the 1950s. Writing in the mid-1970s, the author Leslie Brown observed that 'the onslaught of egg collectors and skin collectors' may have left only four or five surviving pairs. The hills of Carmarthenshire provided a safe home for that remnant population, and thankfully they formed the nucleus of a remarkable comeback.

#### Getting around

Carmarthen and the county's other main towns are linked by good bus services. There are also rail services to Carmarthen, Llanelli and, via the Heart of Wales Line, Llandeilo and Llandovery.

Carmarthenshire's public transport services are patchy beyond the towns, however. Where possible, routes have been chosen that can be reached by train, bus or a combination of the two, but some locations are only accessible by car.

If you do choose to use public transport, please check timings before you set out. Some routes are only served for a day or two a week and, of course, routes and timings will change over time, too.

Traveline Cymru (www.traveline.cymru) is a good source of up-to-date bus and train service information, and it also offers a useful bus stop locator service.

The routes in this guide make use of the county's extensive network of public footpaths, bridleways and other rights of way. In places you will also be walking within areas that are designated as Access Land. The Countryside Rights of Way Act of 2005 created a public right of access on foot to designated Access Land areas. Access Land, *Tir mynediad*, is open country (mountain and moor), common land and forest. On the ground it's indicated by waymarkers – look for a brown logo of a stick man on rolling hills. You can also find access areas marked on the Ordnance Survey's 1:25,000-scale maps.

Wherever you are walking, do take extra care if you take your dog along with you. Farming in Carmarthenshire is all about livestock, and you are likely to come across sheep and cattle on almost every route described in this volume, so it's best to keep dogs on leads, especially during lambing. To give your dog the opportunity to burn off some energy head for the beach. All beaches are open to dogs from October to May. Some, such as the Millennium Coastal Park, remain open to dogs throughout the summer too, while others, such as Pendine and Llansteffan, have dog-free areas from May to the end of September.

### Welsh language

Carmarthenshire, *Sir Gâr*, is a stronghold of the Welsh language. In the whole of Wales about 20 percent of the population can speak Welsh to a greater or lesser degree, but in Carmarthenshire that rises to 44 percent. For the visitor it can help to know a little about the language. Having an understanding of Welsh pronunciation helps with place names, while a few words in Welsh can be a great conversation starter.

*Sounds*
**C** is always hard, like the *c* in cat
**Ch** is like the *ch* in a Scottish loch
**Dd** is like the *th* in the
**F** is like *v* in violin
**Ff** is like the *ff* in off
**Ll** is easy; just place your tongue as though you're going to say 'lord' and then blow
**R** is like the *r* in red, but rolled
**Rh** place your tongue to say the *r* in red and then blow

*Try*
**Bore da** (*Boh-reh dah*): Good morning
**Prynhawn da** (*Prin-houn dah*): Good afternoon
**Iechyd da** (*Yeh-kid dah*): Cheers
**Diolch** (*Dee-olk*): Thank you
**Nos da** (*Nohs dah*): Good night

**To get an idea** of how the Tywi dominates its vast floodplain, it's best to take a bird's-eye view, or something close to it. The top of Merlin's Hill is a good vantage point, as is Paxton's Tower.

One of the great rivers of Wales, the Tywi, or Towy, does a lot in its relatively modest 120km journey from source to sea. From Llandovery to Carmarthen it enjoys its maturity as an almost muscular river that twists and turns across a floodplain flanked by hills.

In winter, the Tywi often rises over its banks and fills low-lying land. It's why the valley's historic river communities, such as Llandeilo and Llanegwad, sit on hills; homes had to be built well away from winter floods.

The valley has always been a highway into Wales. On summer days the caravans that head west on the A40 are following a route once taken by invading armies.

It's probably safe to assume that the inhabitants of Y Garn Goch, the huge hillfort near Llangadog, watched the comings and goings of the Roman legions. The invaders established a port town at what is now Carmarthen.

Later, the valley was a route for incoming Anglo-Norman warlords. Powerful Welsh princes resisted, building castles like Dinefwr – its view of the Tywi landscape is one of the best.

# Tywi Valley

**1. Carmarthen** — 8
Take time out for a teashop break while you explore Wales' oldest town

**2. Merlin's Hill** — 10
Climb to the summit of the hill that's said to have been the home of King Arthur's mentor

**3. Bronwydd** — 12
Some testing gradients to puff your way up on this circular walk to and from Bronwydd Arms

**4. Paxton's Tower** — 14
Feel on top of the world as you take in the panorama from this banker's folly

**5. Llanegwad** — 16
Riverside meadows and views to the hills that are a joy to discover

**6. Aberglasney and Llangathen** — 18
Explore picturesque countryside with an optional foray around a glorious garden

**7. Carreg Cennen** — 20
This great little route delivers varied views of a contender for Carmarthenshire's most romantic ruin

**8. Dinefwr Castle** — 22
Discover a castle that's a close tie for 'most romantic' status, along with classic parkland and lush, cool woods

# Carmarthen

**Distance** 4km **Time** 1 hour **Terrain** urban roads and paths, with steps in places **Map** OS Explorer 177 **Access** good train and bus services to Carmarthen

For a town with close to 2000 years of history to boast about, Carmarthen is surprisingly modest. It doesn't make a fuss about its past, but there's plenty to discover if you take the time.

This exploration of the town starts out from the railway station (alternatively, park at nearby Blue Street car park). From the station's main entrance, go left to walk towards the supporting towers of the suspension footbridge across the Afon Tywi.

The bridge takes you over the wide fast-flowing river to a dual carriageway. Cross the road at the pelican crossing and then turn right. At the roundabout, go left to walk up Blue Street. You'll soon come to the bus station where you climb a flight of stairs on the left to Merlin's Walk Shopping Centre.

Continue along a covered walkway, then go right to walk through the shopping street. On the way you pass a wooden sculpture of Merlin, who is said to have been born in the town.

When you get to Dark Gate, one of the town's oldest thoroughfares, turn right. At the bend where Dark Gate joins Blue Street, cross the road with care, entering Guildhall Square on the other side. The elegant building in the middle of the square ahead of you is the old Guildhall. Built in the 18th century, it functioned as a courthouse until 2016.

Keep to the right-hand side of the square, passing the Guildhall to now follow St Mary's Street to Nott Square.

◀ The Guildhall

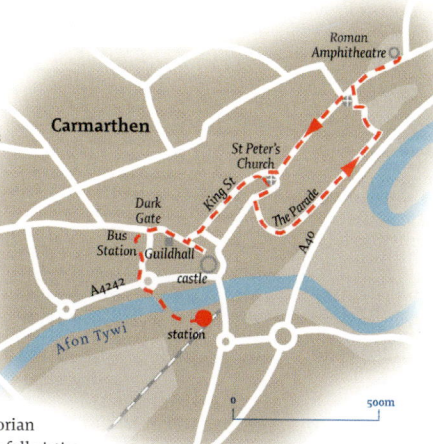

Carry straight on to enter the castle. When the fortress was built in the early 1100s the town's Roman walls were still standing nearby.

Take a moment to explore what remains of the Norman headquarters in Carmarthenshire. It must have been an uncertain life for the community that grew up under the protection of the castle which would, the historian Dylan Rees says, periodically fall victim to 'the vicissitudes of conflict between Welsh and Anglo-Norman forces'. Between 1116 and 1214 the castle was attacked, burned and then repaired five times over.

From the castle, retrace your steps to Nott Square, going right as you leave the castle gate. Walk on to a road junction, where you should keep left to walk along busy King Street, close to the heart of the Roman town.

King Street takes you to the town's parish church, St Peter's. Head inside to see the memorial to Sir Rhys ap Thomas, a local man who played a central role in the creation of the Tudor dynasty. At the end of the Battle of Bosworth Field, in 1485, King Richard III lay dead and Henry Tudor claimed the English throne to become King Henry VII. The blow that felled Richard was dealt by Sir Rhys.

Leave the churchyard by the gate you entered by and then head down Church Lane, past the Oriel Myrddin art gallery, to arrive at busy Church Street. Cross with care to Parade Road.

Here, keep to the footpath on the left. As you head downhill the walkway rises above the level of the road. At the end of Parade Road bear left to walk along The Parade, which later becomes The Esplanade. At the end of The Esplanade, go left onto Old Priory Road.

This brings you to Priory Street. Cross the road and turn right to walk to Carmarthen's Roman amphitheatre. It's surprisingly large, suggesting that events held here attracted an audience from beyond Carmarthen itself.

From the amphitheatre, return along Priory Street to St Peter's, then retrace your steps to the station.

# Merlin's Hill

**Distance** 4.5km **Time** 1 hour 15
**Terrain** footpaths and quiet lanes
**Map** OS Explorer 177 **Access** bus to
Whitemill from Carmarthen

The view from the summit of Merlin's Hill is, appropriately, rather magical. But as you feast your eyes on the surrounding landscape do keep your ears open too; there's a chance you may hear something very unusual.

Was there a real King Arthur? And if so, was his mentor a wizard called Merlin? Possibly, but whether you believe the stories surrounding the Once and Future King have some basis in fact, Carmarthenshire is certain that Merlin was a local boy.

The story goes that he lived out his days bound in chains in a cave on Merlin's Hill. It is said that if you listen carefully you can make out the sound of him rattling his chains.

It's quite a climb to the hilltop (taking you from about 10m above sea level to 150m), including some very steep sections. At one point you'll have to haul yourself up on a rope, but the effort is definitely worth it. You will not see Merlin's cave, of which there's no trace, but you will see the hill's Iron Age fort, which is thought to date back to 400BC. One of the largest forts in West Wales, it was the centre of power at the heart of a large territory.

The starting point for this walk is the parking area on the A40 at White Mill Garage. Alternatively, use the bus to Whitemill, which stops close to the White Mill Inn.

From the garage walk west and then cross the road to walk along the minor road on the far side, which is signposted to Whitemill.

Pass the inn and a postbox, then go right on a footpath that crosses a

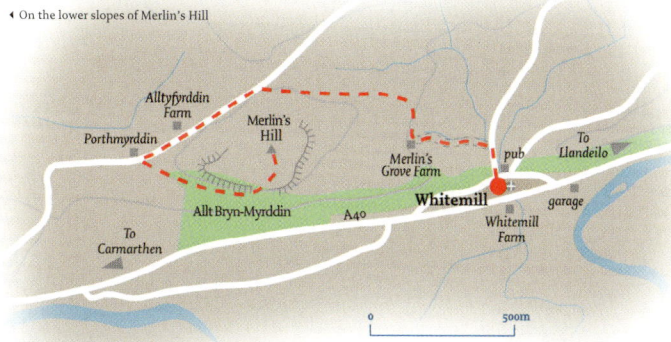

◀ On the lower slopes of Merlin's Hill

footbridge over the Afon Annell. At the road, turn right.

Walk on for 100m to a junction and there go left on a lane that climbs away from the valley. When you reach Merlin's Grove Farm, walk straight on through the farmyard. The track bears right to climb away from the farm buildings.

Stay on this narrow lane (which can be muddy in places) for 500m or so until you arrive at a minor road. Turn left.

You'll soon arrive at Alltyfyrddin Farm, where there's a Merlin-themed visitor centre. Walk on past the farm until you come to the next house, which is called Porthmyrddin (Merlin's Door).

Opposite the house you'll find a kissing gate. Go through the gate and head uphill, staying close to the hedge on your right, to a small gate in the far corner. This opens into a conifer plantation. Enter the woodland, with large beech trees marking the wood's boundary on your right.

As you near the end of the row of beeches, look for an indistinct path between the conifers which bears left to climb the hillside. It's a bit of a scramble as the slope is steep and the hillside is littered with fallen branches. As you go look for a forestry track above you. Head for the track and, when you reach it, go right. Follow the track until you come to a footpath waymark post on the left.

This points the way to a narrow path that climbs the final steep section of the route. A length of rope has been provided to help you up this incline. Beyond the rope, the path levels out a little, but it's still quite a climb through the woodland to a gate. This opens onto grassland.

Go through the gate and bear right to walk past the gorse bushes on your left. Beyond the gorse, turn left to climb the last section of the hill. As you go you'll see an information board ahead, which marks the journey's end. When you've caught your breath (and spent a minute or two listening out for those rattling chains), retrace your steps to Whitemill.

③ TYWI VALLEY

# Bronwydd

**Distance** 8km **Time** 2 hours 30
**Terrain** footpaths and minor roads
**Map** OS Explorer 185 **Access** bus to
Bronwydd from Carmarthen

If you're a steam railway enthusiast this is a great walk to combine with a trip on the Gwili Railway, which keeps open a short stretch of what was once the Great Western's Carmarthen-Aberystwyth Line. If not, it's still worth dropping in to Bronwydd Arms Station to end your visit with tea and cake at the railway's café.

This route begins from the banks of the beautiful Afon Gwili before taking you out of the Gwili Valley into the hills to the west. It's a steady climb.

If you plan to use the railway, start at Bronwydd Arms Station. There's a small museum to explore, and a little café in an old railway carriage. Buy tickets for a train trip from the ticket office on the opposite platform: check opening information in advance. If arriving by car, you can park by the village hall further along the route.

To start your walk head back through the gate and go left to cross the level crossing and head on along the B4301. After 10 minutes or so you will approach a bridge over the Gwili.

As you arrive at the bridge look for a footpath on the left, which is marked by a fingerpost. The path keeps close to the riverbank, passing the village hall and cricket pitch.

From the Gwili's source in the Brechfa Forest to the point where it joins the Tywi at Abergwili is only about 10km as the crow flies. The Gwili takes a rather less direct route, but does it in a rushing tumble. It's worth taking some time to watch the river. It is home to kingfishers and dippers, while in the autumn there are runs of sewin, or sea trout, and

◀ Arriving at Bronwydd Arms Station

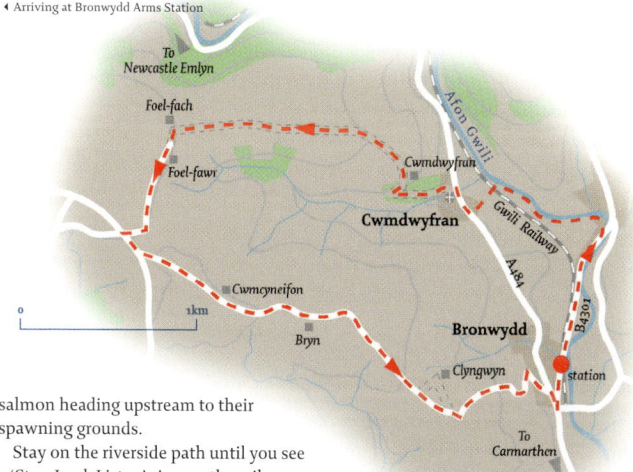

salmon heading upstream to their spawning grounds.

Stay on the riverside path until you see a 'Stop Look Listen' sign on the railway tracks to your left. Walk to the sign and cross the line, then carry on along the field boundary towards the houses ahead.

A small wooden gate opens onto a narrow path alongside a house which brings you to the A484. Go right to walk along the pavement and, in time, cross over at the bus shelter and then continue walking north. Turn left at a chapel to take a narrow lane. You are now in for quite a climb; the lane passes through woodland and in time brings you to a farm called Cwmdwyfran.

Go through the farm's main gate, then immediately turn left to find stone steps that take you over a wall and onto a stony track which continues to climb up the hillside. Stay on the track, which in time becomes a narrow grassy path between tall hedgerows. Further on, the path levels out and the hedges are replaced by wire fences, opening views up across the valley.

When you come to farm buildings at Foel-fâch, go left on a track which leads directly to a second farm, Foel-fawr. Arriving at the buildings of Foel-fawr, keep left to walk along a minor road.

Bear right at a bend in the lane and then left at a junction. Turn left again soon after for a gentle descent into the Gwili Valley. As you go, there's a chance that you'll hear the train whistle in the distance. When you arrive back at the A484, turn right. Then at the next road junction go left to return to Bronwydd Arms Station.

# Paxton's Tower

Distance 5.5km Time 1 hour 30
Terrain footpaths, tracks and roads
Map OS Explorer 186 Access buses to Llanarthne, 1km away

**The view from Paxton's Tower is not to be missed. On a clear day it can seem as though you can see all of Carmarthenshire.**

The landmark tower was built as a memorial to Admiral Horatio Nelson by the owner of Middleton Estate, the very wealthy William Paxton. Born in Berwickshire in 1745, Paxton joined the Royal Navy at the age of 12 as a 'Captain's Boy'. Later he entered the service of the East India Company, rising through the ranks to become the Master of the Mint in Bengal. He returned to Britain in his early 40s with money to burn. Much of it was spent buying, and then improving, Middleton Estate, near Llanarthne, and the tower is the most visible reminder of his influence on his new Welsh home. Completed in 1808, the folly had a banqueting room in which Paxton and his guests could enjoy fine food and views.

The starting point for this walk is the small National Trust car park close to Paxton's Tower. Nearby is a gate to the hilltop field in which the tower stands.

Walk to the tower and go inside to enjoy the view. To the south, you should be able to spot the huge glasshouse that is the centrepiece of the National Botanic Garden of Wales, which now occupies the Middleton Estate. To the north, the Tywi loops and twists across its floodplain, passing this route's second tower, the ruins of Dryslwyn Castle, along the way. It stands on a small crag close to the river.

From the base of Paxton's Tower, take a bearing on Dryslwyn Castle and head on that line across the pasture towards the

◀ Paxton's Tower

wood beyond. The slope is steep.

As you go, look out for a field gate in the fenceline ahead, a little to your right. Head for the gate and go through it onto a track beyond. Bear left to follow the track through woodland. At a waymark post go right.

A little way on, the track brings you to the B4300. Turn right to walk along this road, then left when you come to a crossroads. It's now about 1km to the bridge over the Tywi and the nearby castle. Dryslwyn is thought to have been built in the 1190s, one of many castles constructed in the area over a century or so by both the incoming Normans and native Welsh. One theory is that Dryslwyn was built by Prince Rhys Gryg, Rhys the Hoarse, to protect the Kingdom of Deheubarth. With nearby Dinefwr, it controlled a strategically important east-west route.

After you've explored the castle, retrace your steps over the bridge to the B4300 crossroads. Cross straight over to take a minor road next to the old house on the corner. Pass a second house, bearing right to leave its tarmac drive for a bridleway that begins a long, steady climb.

Keep left where a second track joins from the right, and keep climbing. Along the way the track zigzags and, in time, is sunken, with banks on either side. When you arrive at a minor road, go right. At this point you are about 200m above sea level (and have climbed around 180m since leaving the Dryslwyn crossroads).

Walk on along the lane. After a time you will be able to see the trig point on the summit to your right. When you come to a junction, go right. The lane passes a cottage, then heads through a belt of woodland before bringing you back to your starting point.

# Llanegwad

Distance 4km Time 1 hour
Terrain footpaths, farm tracks and minor roads Map OS Explorer 186
Access bus to Llanegwad from Carmarthen and Llandeilo

This is a great Tywi Valley walk at any time of year, but is especially good in winter. When the trees are leafless, the views to the low-lying floodplain are that bit bigger. The landscape changes from day to day as the river shrinks and grows from season to season. After floods, the fields become ponds and lakes before draining away when the weather turns drier.

This walk sticks to a small island of higher ground close to the main Carmarthen to Llandeilo road (A40). The starting point is the centre of Llanegwad, close to the parish church (where there is some on-road parking). The church that you see today isn't that old – it was built in the 19th century – but stonework was re-used from an earlier building that is thought to have dated back to the 11th century.

With your back to the churchyard gate, go right to walk along the main village road, which bears left. Where the road makes a sharp bend to the right look out for a footpath sign on your left.

Taking this path, which runs along the side of a garden, you soon come to a stile. Climb this and walk straight on along the line of the hedge on your right to a second

◀ St Egwad's Church

stile on the far side of the field.

Go over the stile and head straight on to a minor road. Walk directly across the road to a farm track, which leads away from the village. As you head west there are good views over the river valley. Look out too for a tree-topped hillock in a field on the left – it's a motte-and-bailey castle called Pen y Cnap. The little stronghold may have been an outpost for the garrison at Dryslwyn, 4km to the east.

Walk on along the track for 10 minutes or so until you arrive at a farm called Kincoed. The track takes you on through the farmyard before dropping downhill through woodland. You soon come to a country lane and, on the far side, the Afon Cothi, a tributary of the Tywi.

Turn left to walk along the lane, which soon begins to bear left to take you back towards Llanegwad, passing Abercothi House along the way. In time the road nears a long stone bridge – just before you reach it, look for a footpath sign on a telephone pole on your left. It points the way to a track.

Cross a cattle grid to walk along the track heading for a farm, Llwchgwyn, which you will soon see ahead. At the farm, cross the yard and head on east along the track, which climbs towards Llanegwad. When you arrive back at the village street go right to return to your starting point by the church.

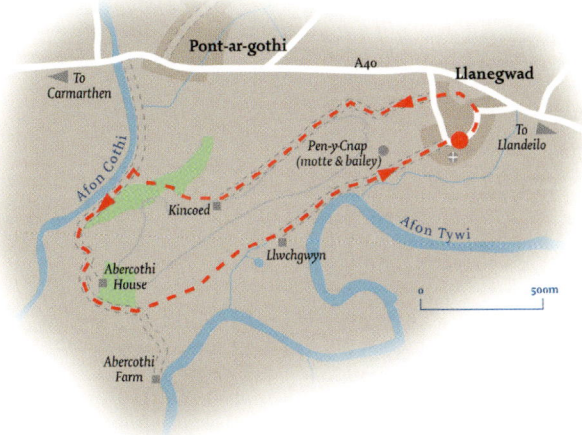

# Aberglasney and Llangathen

**Distance** 2.5km **Time** 15 minutes
**Terrain** country lanes, farmland paths
**Map** OS Explorer 186 **Access** bus to
Aberglasney (Broad Oak stop) from
Carmarthen and Llandovery

There's a fairytale feel to the story of
Carmarthenshire's sleeping beauty,
Aberglasney. In the years before the
Second World War, the medieval house
was a family home but it was abandoned
by the 1950s.

Unoccupied for decades, Aberglasney
House crumbled while its gardens became
a tangled wilderness. Fortunately, a
charity, the Aberglasney Restoration
Trust, came to the rescue in the late 1990s,
saving the house and restoring the
gardens to their former glory. The gardens
are worth a visit at any time of year but
are at their very best in spring.

This short walk around Llangathen
is perfect as an add-on to a visit to
Aberglasney. Start your journey from the
turning to Aberglasney (with your back
to the house) and turn right to walk
towards Llangathen.

You'll soon pass a large mock tudor
building on your right, which is
Llangathen Village Hall. It was built in
1906 by the Aberglasney Estate as a
temperance hall providing villagers with
wholesome, alcohol-free entertainment.

Walk on, looking out for the solid 15th-
century tower of the village church on the
skyline to your left. On your left you'll see
a kissing gate in the hedge. Go through
the gate and cross a small field towards
the church – head to the kissing gate that
opens into St Cathen's churchyard.

◀ The 15th-century tower of St Cathen's

Walk through the churchyard, passing to the right of the church to reach a gate on the far side. Leave St Cathen's through this and turn right to walk along a minor road, passing Berllan Dywyll Farm (*berllan* is the Welsh word for 'orchard'). When you reach a junction, go left.

Continue for 500m with woodland on either side of you. Where the lane goes round a sharp bend look out for a stile in the hedge on your left. Climb over the stile into a field and head up the slope, keeping close to a wood on your left. As you go take a moment to appreciate the view to the east over the Tywi. The Black Mountain on the skyline makes the perfect backdrop for Dinefwr Castle, which tops a wooded hill 2km away.

Walking on you'll soon pass the wood. To your left the steep slope rises to a row of veteran oaks (in a field hedge that's just out of sight).

Bear left to climb the slope towards the hedge. Getting closer, you will see a tall stile close to the base of one of the big oaks. When you reach the stile, climb over it, and then over a second stile close by. Head right to walk on uphill towards a lone cottage.

Opposite the cottage there's a gate and stile. Go over the stile to the minor road and turn left to walk back to Llangathen. Keep left at the first junction you come to and right at the next. When you arrive at a T-junction, go right to walk back to the Aberglasney entrance.

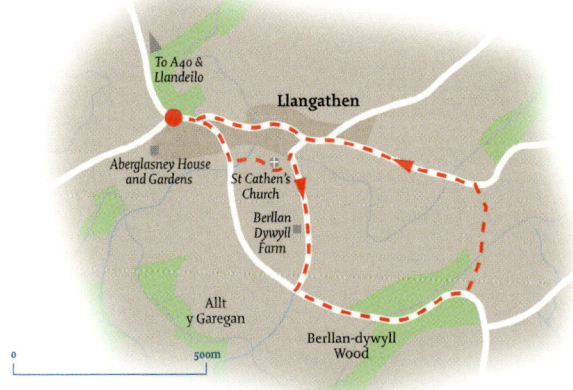

# Carreg Cennen

**Distance** 3.5km **Time** 1 hour
**Terrain** woodland paths, steep in places, and minor roads **Map** OS Explorer 186
**Access** the nearest train station is at Ffairfach, a 5km walk on the Beacons Way to the start

**Against some pretty stiff competition, Carreg Cennen Castle has to be Carmarthenshire's most romantic ruin, which is why it has been attracting visitors since at least the 18th century.**

One of those 18th-century travellers who made the journey to see the hilltop fortress was the landscape painter J M W Turner. In his watercolour the castle is a brooding silhouette against a storm-driven sky of moody greys and browns.

Whatever the weather, Carreg Cennen is an imposing sight. Built on, and into, a limestone crag, it's visible for miles around. It is thought to date back to the late 12th century, when it was built to defend the Welsh kingdom of Deheubarth. Later it was strengthened after England's King Edward I granted Carreg Cennen to a loyal supporter, John Giffard. In 1403 the stronghold was involved in the bid for Welsh independence led by Owain Glyndwr. Repairs to the castle's walls had to be carried out after they had been 'destroyed and thrown down' by Glyndwr's forces.

Half a century later the castle was again drawn into a conflict – this time the civil war known as the Wars of the Roses.

# Carreg Cennen

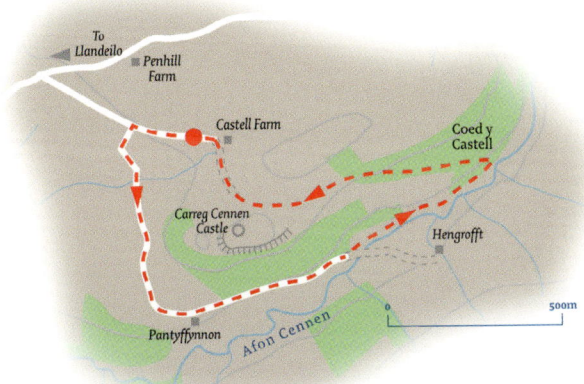

It was a base for Lancastrian forces and no one dared approach, knowing it was occupied 'by rebels and robbers to the destruction of the country round'.

This short walk through that countryside is a great way to get a feel for the landscape the castle has dominated for at least seven centuries. Along the way you'll pass the entrance and Cadw ticket office, and it's definitely worth taking time out to explore inside the walls.

Leave the castle's car park through the main gate and walk along the approach road. (Take note of when the gates shut if walking later in the day.) At the first junction you come to, go left to take a minor road that drops into a valley and then passes below the castle crag.

Stay on the road for about 1km. In time you will arrive at a trio of field gates – one straight ahead and the others either side. Pick the one in the middle, passing through the kissing gate alongside it to enter Coed y Castell. The path takes you through mature woodland which is alive with birdsong in spring and summer.

At a waymark post go straight on along a footpath, which follows the line of the Cennen on your right, and continue to a series of steps that lead to a stile by a waymark post.

Climb over the stile and go right to walk on below impressive old oak trees. When you arrive at a footbridge over the Cennen don't cross it; instead, keep left to join the Beacons Way and begin the climb towards the castle gate.

Soon you're looking down on the treetops in the valley below and there are great views to the south and east.

A little further on and you will see the castle ahead of you. At the castle entrance keep straight on along the Beacons Way, which takes you to Castell Farm. Go straight on through the farmyard to return to the castle car park.

◀ Carreg Cennen Castle

# Dinefwr Castle

**Distance** 4km **Time** 1 hour 15
**Terrain** footpaths, woodland paths, some steps **Map** OS Explorer 186
**Access** bus to Llandeilo or nearest train station is at Ffairfach, 1km from the start

**Whoever chose the site of Dinefwr Castle had an eye for landscape. The views from its commanding position above the Tywi Valley are huge and more than repay the effort it takes to get to the top of its tallest tower.**

Start out from the bottom end of Llandeilo's Bridge Street by walking towards the bridge across the Tywi. Just before reaching it, turn right into a narrow lane. It takes you past a row of cottages and the Dynevor Estate's South Lodge.

As you go it's worth taking a moment to look back at the elegant single-span bridge. It was completed in 1847 after years of difficulties. An optimist called Morgan Morgan won the contract to build it as lowest bidder, but his budget of £6000 was spent on the foundations alone. He was sacked and the final bill topped £21,000.

Heading on, you soon arrive at a pair of gates. Go through the one on the right to enter Castle Wood Nature Reserve. Follow the path that heads up into woodland. Keep left at the first junction of paths and right at the second junction.

You're soon walking with metal railings on your left. Where the railings come to an end, take the path on your left, which doubles back and descends stone steps. The path brings you into the churchyard of Llandyfeisant. The church dates from the 19th century, but it stands on the site of a much earlier building.

Head right to go round the back of the church to its front entrance, then continue to a gate in the boundary wall.

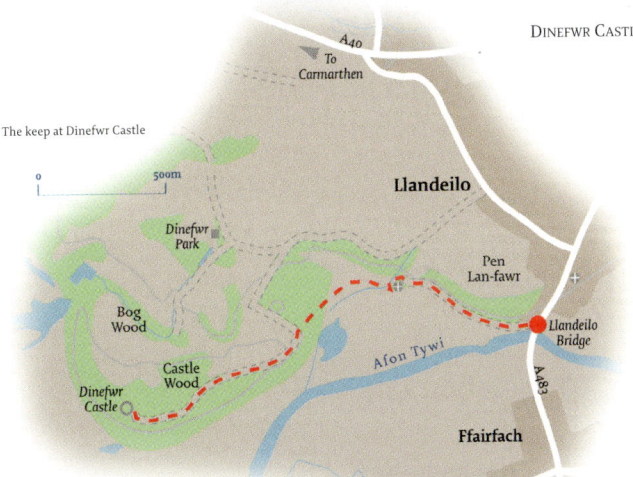

◀ The keep at Dinefwr Castle

Go through the gate and bear right to pass through a smaller second gate.

Follow the line of the churchyard wall to a large drinking trough, which is fed by a tiny stream. Then, with your back to the trough, walk straight ahead across close-cropped grass, aiming for a veteran oak tree in the field in front of you.

As you get closer to the oak, bear left towards the field boundary and follow it as you climb a gentle slope towards distant woodland. In time you will come to a small gate that takes you into a second large field. Keep left to walk on to another small gate which leads into woodland. Follow the path to a third gate and on into an area of open parkland.

Walk uphill, keeping close to the fence on your left. It soon joins a track where you should go left and continue to a gate with a 'Castle Woods Nature Reserve' sign. Enter the reserve and head straight on through what is an ancient woodland; in spring the show of bluebells and other woodland flowers, such as wood anemone, is hard to beat.

At a path junction go left to join a track that continues to climb the hill. You soon arrive at the castle. Dinefwr was a court for the Princes of Deheubarth, whose power extended to most of South Wales. The castle was a particular favourite of the greatest of the Deheubarth princes, Lord Rhys, who ruled for half a century until his death in 1197.

While you're on the battlements look to the north to see Newton House, which replaced the castle in the 17th century. During the 18th century the castle was used by the Newton House family as their very grand summerhouse.

When it's time to head home, retrace your steps to Llandyfeisant Church and on to Bridge Street.

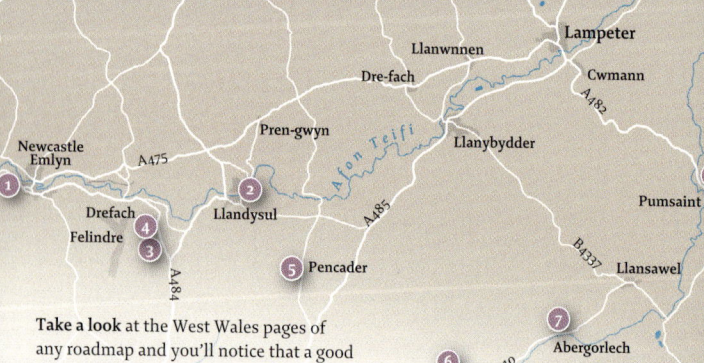

**Take a look** at the West Wales pages of any roadmap and you'll notice that a good portion of the north of the county is relatively empty. There are as many rivers as roads. It's just the place to get off the beaten track; the north's thinly-populated hills and forests are a joy to explore.

For much of its middle section the brisk, fast-moving Teifi forms Carmarthenshire's northern border. Where the river tumbles over falls at Cenarth you can stand on the village's old bridge and have a foot in Carmarthenshire and another in Ceredigion.

It's a similar situation at lots of other Teifi Valley communities, including Llandysul and Newcastle Emlyn. Each owes its existence to its bridge.

More modest rivers have had a big influence on other communities. Drefach and Felindre were once known throughout Wales and beyond for the quality of the woollen cloth produced at their water-powered mills.

Also, don't miss the area's unlikeliest bit of industrial heritage – its goldmine. As far back as Roman times, gold was being extracted by the Cothi at Pumsaint.

# North

**1  Newcastle Emlyn and Cenarth**  26
You're never far from the Teifi on this walk through rolling farmland and peaceful woods

**2  Pont-Tyweli and Llandysul**  28
Pick up a picnic in town and then head for the hills above two great rivers

**3  Drefach and Drefelin**  30
Explore quiet wooded valleys that once rang to the clatter of water-driven woollen mills

**4  Nant Esgair**  32
Step into the past on this gentle walk to discover peaceful woodland, mills and chapels

**5  Pencader**  34
A short walk, but quite a climb to impressive views to the east of Brechfa Forest

**6  Keepers Walk**  36
Get a taste of the Brechfa experience on this easy-going stroll in the former Royal Forest

**7  Abergorlech**  38
A woodland walk in the picturesque Cothi Valley that begins and ends at one of the area's best-loved inns

**8  Dolaucothi Gold Mine**  40
Combine a tour of the Roman site with this great walk for the perfect underground-overground day out

# Newcastle Emlyn and Cenarth

**Distance** 4.4km **Time** 1 hour (one-way)
**Terrain** bridleways, farm tracks and woodland paths; steep in places
**Map** OS Explorer 185 **Access** return by bus to Newcastle Emlyn from Cenarth (no Sunday service; check timetable before setting out)

You can't fail to be impressed by the sheer power of the Teifi as it thunders over the series of falls just upriver from the bridge at Cenarth. When the river is in spate the falls are spectacular. They're the end point for this short walk between Teifi neighbours Newcastle Emlyn and Cenarth, a village that sits half in Carmarthenshire and half in Ceredigion.

Like all market towns, the cattle market is the beating heart of Newcastle Emlyn. If you are there on a Thursday, which is market day, you'll find the town's Cattle Market car park buzzing with activity. Parking spaces can be hard to find, but on other days it's much quieter. The starting point for this short walk is the town's main bus stop, which is at the car park's entrance on New Road.

With your back to the bus shelter, start off by going right to walk along New Road, passing the fire station, to reach a junction with the A484 Carmarthen-Cardigan road. Go right here to head along the pavement on the right-hand side of the road. Soon after a postbox (on the opposite side), look for a turning on the left, just before a church with a small spire. Cross the road here.

Walk a short way uphill on this minor road to a waymark post. Go right here to take the lane which in time leads to Gelligatti Farm with its impressive listed stone farmhouse. Stay on the lane to continue by the farmhouse, passing through two gates along the way to arrive

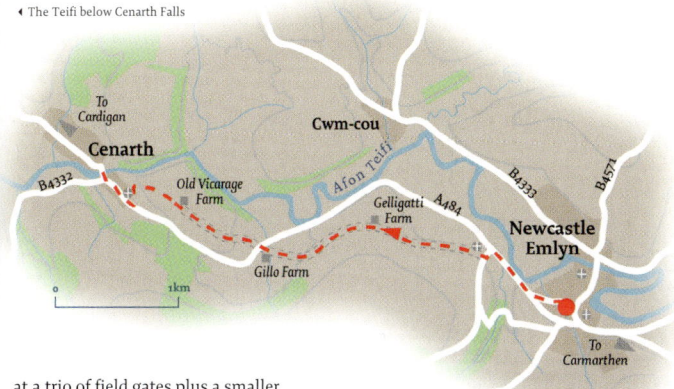

◀ The Teifi below Cenarth Falls

at a trio of field gates plus a smaller waymarked gate. Go through the small gate to walk on between veteran beech, ash and oak trees. At a gate with a waymark, pass on through and carry on downhill along the narrow footpath.

This takes you to the right of outbuildings at Gillo Farm after which you should go right at the farm's drive to walk a short way to the A484. Take care crossing the busy road to get to the lane on the far side. Head up this lane to climb away from the A484. You soon come to a waymark post where you should go left onto a green lane.

Stay on this narrow bridleway to climb steadily until the gradient eases near Old Vicarage Farm. Go straight on to pass the farm and reach a field gate with a smaller gate close by. Head through the small gate into a field and take the path that follows the line of the hedge west towards Cenarth. After a short distance you will see the tower of St Llawddog's Church.

Go through a small gate and turn left to follow a minor road that skirts the churchyard and brings you back to the A484. Turn right. Take note that the stop for buses to Newcastle Emlyn is just by the churchyard gate, but carry straight on past this to spend a little time exploring Cenarth before you head back to Emlyn.

The falls, which can be accessed from the bridge further down this road, are particularly impressive after a few days of rain. Cross to the far side and turn right for the viewing platform and riverside path. If you spend time watching the tumble of whitewater in autumn there's a chance you'll see fish jumping; sea trout battle against the river flow to get to spawning grounds upriver.

# Pont-Tyweli and Llandysul

Distance 8km Time 2 hours
Terrain woodland paths, roads and farm paths Map OS Explorer 185 Access buses to Llandysul from Carmarthen

For much of its course the Afon Teifi is the border between counties, and at Pont-Tyweli it effectively splits a town down the middle. So, your starting point for this Carmarthenshire walk – the car park at Llandysul's St Tysul's Church – is actually in Ceredigion.

From the car park go up steps by the public toilet block and turn left to walk west along Church Street, which becomes New Road. Keep left at its junction with Bridge Street to head onto the bridge over the Teifi.

Cross to Carmarthenshire. The road bends right before coming to a junction, where you should turn left onto Pencader Road. After passing the garage, go left onto Morris Terrace and continue. When you reach the last house, carry straight on, ignoring the road joining from the right. After around 1km, at Dol-llan Farm, keep right at the fork.

The road climbs steadily before looping to the right, following the meandering course of the Teifi. Look out for a wooded hill to the east – its hillfort is said to have been the last home of Vortigern, the 5th-century king who is a recurring character in the Arthurian legends.

Walking on, look out for a waymark sign and gate on your right just before you reach Fron-gôch Farm. From the gate, head up the hillside towards a field gate that's behind, and above, farm buildings.

Go through the gate and on along a track, which takes you towards a hedge on the brow of the hill. As you get closer to the hedge, bear right to a kissing gate in the corner of the field and carry on into the next field.

Head towards a pair of field gates on the

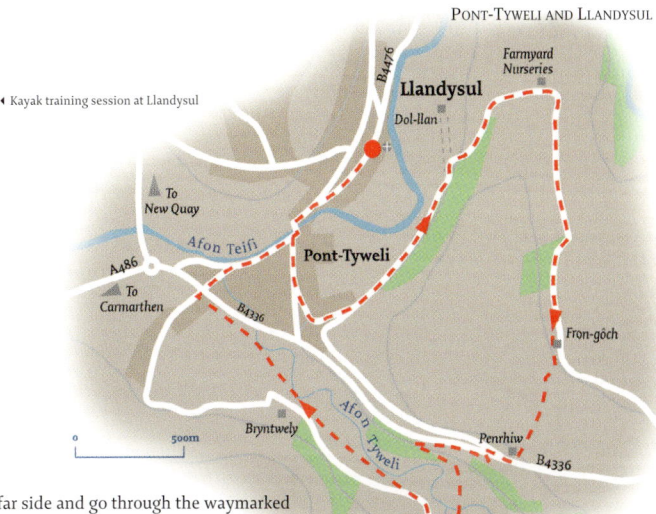

◀ Kayak training session at Llandysul

far side and go through the waymarked gate on the right. Head downhill on a farm track that takes you through the farmyard at Penrhiw to the B4336.

Turn right and keep to the verge on the right-hand side of the B4336, ignoring the smaller lane branching off to the right. A little further on you'll see a footpath sign and gate on the opposite side.

Go through this gate and descend the wooded valleyside. The path bears left for a short distance to a waymark post before turning sharply right to head towards the Afon Tyweli. At the next junction of paths (at a waymark post) go left. When you come to the edge of the woodland head diagonally across the river meadow to a small footbridge.

Cross the bridge and bear right to a gate opening onto what was the trackbed of the Carmarthen & Cardigan Railway, which closed in the 1950s. Cross to a second small gate. After passing through this, walk along the bank of a stream towards a cottage. A gate opposite the cottage opens onto a minor road.

Turn right to walk along this lane. You'll soon come to a footpath sign on your right, where a kissing gate opens onto the disused line. Pass through the gate and head left. Stay on the old line for the next 1km or so as it follows the course of the Afon Tyweli.

In time you'll see the raised section of the B4336. The path narrows and after a while passes a house and brings you to a kissing gate, which opens onto a road.

Go right to cross a bridge above the B4336 and walk on into Pont-Tyweli. At a T-junction by a pub go right; it's then a short walk back to the Teifi bridge.

# Drefach and Drefelin

Distance 5km Time 1 hour 30
Terrain footpaths, minor roads
Map OS Explorer 185 Access bus to
Drefach from Newcastle Emlyn,
Carmarthen and Cardigan

**Drefach and Felindre, and their
neighbouring hamlets, were once the
powerhouse of the Welsh woollen
industry. In wool's heyday there were
scores of woollen mills in the area,
employing hundreds of local men,
women and children.**

This walk and the next both start and finish at Cambrian Mills, which was one of the area's biggest employers but is now home to the excellent National Wool Museum (free entry). A must for anyone with an interest in social history, it's a gem of a museum. It remembers a time when the area was nicknamed 'The Huddersfield of Wales'. In its heyday there were more than 170 water-powered mills and workshops turning raw wool into high-quality cloth in this area. An intricate network of footpaths were used by locals to get to work and, on the week's one day of rest, to chapel.

Begin your walk at the museum. Leaving via the main gate, turn right onto the road through Drefach and then immediately right again to take a waymarked footpath that leads along the boundary of the museum site to a bridge over the Nant Bargod.

Cross the bridge and walk along an

avenue, with tall closely-spaced pines on both sides. The large house that you pass on your right was once the home of one of the mill owners.

When you come to a sharp bend to the right, bear left to take a narrow path which soon brings you to a minor road. Turn left here. After passing a row of small bungalows and the 'Pwllmarl' street sign, go left onto a track. The track, a public right of way, is the drive to Pwllmarl Farm.

At the farmyard go straight on to a narrow concrete path and then a kissing gate by a footbridge. Cross the bridge and continue to the village main street. Turn right. As you walk you will pass the imposing Bethel Chapel and then a fine Victorian house named Meiros Hall. It was the home of the owner of nearby Meiros Mill.

At the road junction turn left to walk uphill until you approach a cemetery, then go right to take a lane marked as a no-through way. Look out for a small house on the left called Dolwion Cottage. Close by is Dolwion Mill, one of the area's first factories. It was once owned by close relatives of not one, but two US Presidents – John Adams and his son John Quincy Adams.

From Dolwion Cottage, stay on the tarmac road, passing other cottages and looking out for a narrow concrete path (with a handrail) on your right. Take this path, which drops down to the river.

At an outbuilding go left and walk on to reach the bridge at Drefelin, then head left to walk along the village street. In time the road leaves Drefelin and heads towards Clos y graig Methodist Chapel. Before you reach the chapel go left to take a minor road that climbs steeply out of the valley.

After 350m you arrive at the hamlet of Cefncanol. Take a moment to enjoy the impressive views across Felindre, then go left. It's now a 750m walk along the road back down into Drefach. When you arrive at the village main street go right to retrace your steps to the museum.

◀ Bethel Baptist Chapel

# Nant Esgair

Distance **6.8km** Time **2 hours**
Terrain **woodland paths and minor roads** Map **OS Explorer 185**
Access **bus to Drefach from Carmarthen and Newcastle Emlyn**

**Cloth-making in the valleys that converge at Felindre started as a cottage industry. Later, large water-driven mills were built along the Nant Bargod, Nant Esgair and Nant Brân.**

This route takes you along the valley of Nant Esgair from Drefach. Once again the starting point is the National Woollen Museum; at the main gate (with your back to the building) go right to walk through the village.

At the junction near St Barnabas Church turn right and then cross the road to go left on a minor road. Walk along the line of the churchyard wall, passing a metal gate to reach a second gate on your left. Go through this and take a footpath into hazel woodland, which is full of bluebells in spring. When you come to a junction of paths, keep left and follow this path until you reach two wooden gates roughly 20 paces apart. Pass through both gates and head straight on to a third gate. Go through this last gate and bear left to a stile into a field. Head on, keeping close to the hedge on your left. There are powerlines overhead.

Where the powerlines cross the field, follow the same line to a small gate by a footbridge. Cross the bridge and then head straight on to a track, where you bear left. You will soon reach the Felindre-Cwmpengraig road. Go right and stay on the road for about 1.5km to Cwmpengraig.

Along the way you'll pass an interesting mix of houses, including the thatched Ffatri yr Ogof. This was once a family textile business.

Pass a phonebox. Then take the first turning on the right and head down to

◀ Ffatri yr Ogof was once a small-scale mill

a small bridge over the Nant Esgair and reach the imposing Soar Chapel.

Bear left. Just after the road passes the last house, look out for a flight of steps on the right. Climb these and walk on into woodland. Stay on the path along the valley above Cwmpengraig. In time you will come to a gate. Go through the gate and bear right to pass through a second, before bearing left to head on along the woodland path.

At another flight of concrete steps, go left to climb to a narrow path which zigzags through the woodland. It brings you to a stile that's within sight of Penlangribin Farm. Climb over the stile and, with it at your back, go straight on along the line of a hedge. Walk on to another stile.

Climb over the stile and go left along the farm track. After about 200m look out for a kissing gate on your right, which is half hidden in the hedge. Go through this gate into a field. Walk along the line of the hedge that's on your right to the field's corner, where another gate opens onto a road. Turn right to walk along a lane, passing a bungalow along the way. The next property you come to is a cottage close to a bend in the road.

Opposite the cottage look for a waymark post by a field gate, which has a kissing gate alongside it. Go through the kissing gate to walk along the line of the hedge that's on your right, heading towards powerline poles near a woodland.

When you reach the wood you will see a stile. Climb over it then walk on along a woodland path to reach another minor road. Go right and stay on this road to return to St Barnabas Church. Retrace your steps to the start.

## 5 NORTH

# Pencader

**Distance** 6km **Time** 1 hour 30
**Terrain** quiet roads, farm tracks and paths; steep in places **Map** OS Explorer 185
**Access** bus to Pencader from Carmarthen and Aberystwyth

Pencader is a little out of the way, but it has had its moment in history. In his day, King Henry II of England ruled an empire that stretched from the Scottish border all the way to Aquitaine, but controlling Wales gave him trouble.

If you believe the story of the Old Man of Pencader, Henry was once given some straight-talking advice about Wales and the Welsh while in Pencader. It's said that Henry got into conversation with a man he met on the road in Pencader when he was on the way to Cardigan to meet Lord Rhys, Prince of Deheubarth. The villager told him that Wales could be defeated by man, but only destroyed by God, and added that on the Day of Judgement someone speaking Welsh would answer 'the Supreme Judge for this small corner of the earth'. What Henry said in reply was not recorded, but he did give Lord Rhys a relatively free hand in ruling Deheubarth.

This short walk starts out from the heart of the village, where there is space to park at the recreation ground. From the recreation ground entrance go left and then cross the B4459 to a minor road, Castle Road, on the far side.

Follow Castle Road, which soon passes Yr Hen Capel (The Old Chapel) before crossing a river and beginning to climb the hillside. As you go, the raised area to your right is the site of Pencader's castle.

It is thought to have been built in the 1140s for Gilbert de Clare, the Earl of Pembroke, during a push east into Deheubarth. The Welsh soon chased

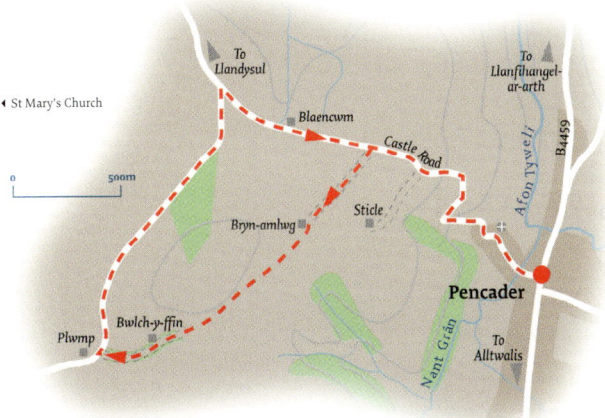

◀ St Mary's Church

de Clare's men out, and the castle was a Deheubarth stronghold when King Henry came to call in the 1160s.

Soon after passing the castle site you will come to St Mary's Church, which stands back from the road behind a row of cottages. Head on along Castle Road.

The coming 1km or so is quite a climb. Take time along the way to stop and enjoy the impressive view to the east; the wind turbines on the horizon are part of the huge Brechfa Forest Wind Farm.

In time the gradient eases up. Pass the gate to Sticle Estate and head on, looking out for a footpath fingerpost on the left which points the way to a small metal gate. Go through this gate and continue a short way to a track, which leads to a house named Bryn-amlwg. Bear left to follow this track towards the house ahead of you. When you reach the point where the track swings right to the house, pass through a waymarked gate on your left.

Head on along the narrow path which soon brings you to a stile. Climb over the stile into a large field and walk on, keeping close to the hedge on your left.

Stay on the same southwesterly line, passing a field gate (on your left) and continuing to a second gateway. Go through this gate and, still bearing southwest, walk towards the trees that you can see ahead of you.

When you reach the trees you'll see a narrow lane between tree-lined banks. Follow the lane, passing derelict farm buildings as you go. Go through the gate across the lane and then continue for 300m to a minor road. Turn right to take this road for about 15 minutes, passing a conifer plantation before arriving at a junction where you turn right again.

You will soon reach the point where you first left Castle Road to walk towards Bryn-amlwg. From here, retrace your steps to your starting point.

# Keepers Walk

**Distance** 2.5km **Time** 45 minutes
**Terrain** forest paths and tracks
**Map** OS Explorer 186 **Access** buses from Carmarthen and Brechfa

Over its long, long history, Brechfa Forest has served a number of purposes. It has been a hunting ground for the nobility and a timber 'factory' for the nation, but is now something of a playground for mountain bikers. As a result there are lots of first-class biking routes, while it also has plenty of space for walkers to explore. This walk is the perfect introduction to the Brechfa experience.

In the Middle Ages much of what is now Brechfa Forest was the Forest of Glyn Cothi, a royal forest. These days we understand the word 'forest' in a very different way to how the word was used in medieval times. Then, it would have been a hunting ground, reserved for kings and landowning nobles. Strict forest-wide laws applied and locals faced severe punishments if they were caught taking 'venison'. At the time venison was used as a catch-all term for the meat of any woodland animal. So hunting anything furry – deer, boar, wolf or fox – was a risky business for anyone without royal connections.

The forest lost its royal protection in the 17th century. Today's Brechfa Forest is relatively young; it was created by the Forestry Commission after the First World War as part of a national drive to meet Britain's timber needs without imports. These days the forest's 6500 hectares are managed by the Welsh government. Public access is excellent – there's lots of space – but the best way to begin to explore (without getting lost) is to use one of a number of waymarked routes, such as Keepers Walk. This begins and

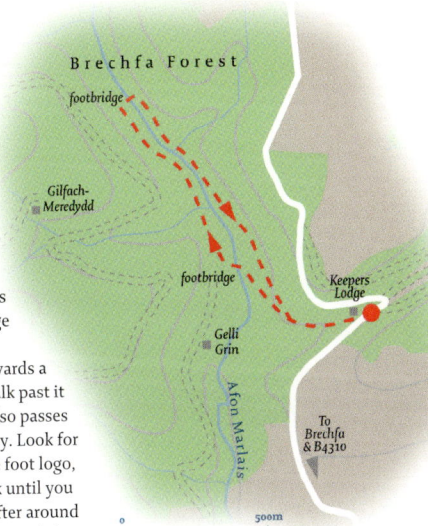

◀ A woodland footbridge

ends at the car park at Keepers Lodge, just north of the village of Brechfa.

From the car park, head towards a large open-sided barn and walk past it to take a forest track which also passes a vehicle barrier along the way. Look for a waymarker post with a blue foot logo, then continue along the track until you see a second waymark post after around 50m. When you reach the post, go left to take a narrow path that heads downhill between tall conifers.

Stay on this path as it drops down the valleyside towards the Afon Marlais, which you will hear before you can see it. At another waymark post, the path swings to the left to bring you to a wooden footbridge over the river. In summer this bridge can look a little out of scale given the modest size of the Marlais, but when the river is in flood after heavy rain it swells to become a torrent. Cross the bridge and stay on the path to climb away from the river. The route zigzags through conifers and then hazels.

Go straight on at one waymark post and then again at a second. The path swings to the right before zigzagging again to bring you to a second footbridge. Cross the bridge and walk straight on to come, in time, to a track where you go right. When this track emerges at a big open junction, go right to cross the Marlais once again. Look out for the next waymark post where you go right on a narrow path down to the riverbank.

Head on along the Marlais, crossing a footbridge close to a bench. The path then climbs through the woods to a forest track. Go right to walk back to the car park.

# Abergorlech

Distance 2.5km Time 45 minutes
Terrain forest paths and roads
Map OS Explorer 186 Access buses to Abergorlech from Llandeilo

Abergorlech is a quiet village at an old bridging point over the Afon Cothi. Way back in the 17th century it was one of a number of Carmarthenshire villages that had a fulling mill, which in a small way made it a centre of industry.

Fulling is one of the stages in the process of making raw wool into cloth. At a fulling mill, wool was washed to remove oil and dirt, and was worked with water-driven hammers to increase its volume. The Welsh word for a fulling mill is *pandy* and it occasionally turns up in place names – Tonypandy is an example. The mill is long gone and these days it's the tourism industry that keeps Abergorlech busy.

One of Brechfa Forest's most popular car parks is at the eastern end of the village, and it's the starting point for a number of walking and biking trails that explore the forest. This short walk provides a taste of that forest experience. You can follow Natural Resources Wales' waymarked routes if you'd like to explore further.

The walk starts at the village pub, The Black Lion, which stands close to the 19th-century church, St David's. (For drivers, parking is available at the Natural Resources Wales car park at the eastern end of the village – the route passes through this.) From the pub, begin walking along the B4310, taking care as there is no pavement. You will soon come to the stone bridge over the Gorlech,

◀ Walking a forest track

which flows into the Cothi close by. The *aber* in Abergorlech means the 'mouth of'. After crossing the bridge look for the Natural Resources Wales car park on the left. Go into the car park and then walk on through it to a striking carved tree trunk.

Carry on walking along the track that passes the carving and takes you through a second car park. Stay on the track as it climbs gently away from the car park, and look for a waymark post which is marked with routes for three trails – yellow, blue and purple. Go left to a gate and then head straight on to a footbridge that spans the Gorlech.

The Gorlech is little more than a stream, but it is used by salmon and sewin (sea trout). In autumn they swim up the Cothi to spawn and continue on into the Gorlech, laying their eggs on gravel in the riverbed. Cross the bridge, then stay on the riverbank path heading into the forest until you come to a second footbridge with a striking humpback design.

This footbridge takes you back over the Gorlech where you then bear right to return to the main forest track. Stay on the track to reach the B4310 and walk back to The Black Lion.

If you would like to venture further from the humpback bridge, try following the Forest Garden Walk (purple waymarking). This takes you deep into the forest to an area where foresters did some experimental planting in the 1950s. Tree species from around the world were planted to see how they would do in the Brechfa climate. They include conifers, such as giant redwood, and deciduous trees, such as South American beech.

# Dolaucothi Gold Mine

Distance 5.5km Time 1 hour 30
Terrain footpaths, woodland tracks and paths; steep in places Map OS Explorer 186
Access no public transport to the start

No-one knows how, or when, the Romans got to know that there was gold to be found in the hills of Carmarthenshire, but there's a chance that it was one reason for their push west. Before 80AD, a fort had been built at Pumsaint and gold mining began soon after on an industrial scale. Tunnels, or adits, were cut to get to veins of ore, and opencast pits were dug too. The workings, and the surrounding Dolaucothi Estate, are now a National Trust property. Combine this enjoyable walk – which uses public footpaths and National Trust permissive paths – with a mine visit for a great day out.

Start out from the car park opposite the main entrance to the mine. At the end of the car park that's furthest from the road, take the path waymarked as the red trail. You're soon walking above the Afon Cothi. Head through a gate and then go left to reach a bridge over the river. Cross the bridge, then bear right on the far side. At a waymark post go left (following a yellow trail direction arrow). You'll soon come to a second waymark post next to a stone wall.

Bear left and walk on to a kissing gate. Head on through the gate towards a footbridge ahead. Cross the bridge and climb a short flight of steps to a waymark point, continuing straight on here.

At the next waymark post, go left (red trail) to walk to the next junction, where you join a track that runs east-west along the valley. Go right – you'll see Dolaucothi Farm over to the east (on your right).

After about 400m look out for a stile on the right. Climb over the stile and follow the line of the hedge to the corner

# DOLAUCOTHI GOLD MINE

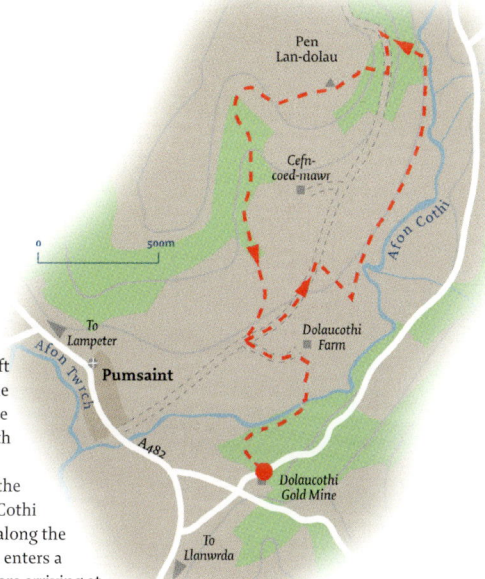

◀ A view to the Cothi

of the field. At the corner, make a 90-degree turn to your left to again skirt along the field boundary. For the next 1km or so the path takes you on a near-straight course along the valley side above the Cothi (see red trail markers along the way). In time the path enters a conifer plantation before arriving at a forest track.

At the track, go left. It's quite a climb before the gradient begins to level out. Look out for a waymark post where you go left. Walk on to a second waymark post, where you should go right to leave the track before soon coming to a third waymark post. Go left here.

Climb out of the valley to a gate that takes you out onto open hillside. Ahead you'll see a triangulation point, or pillar, on the hill's summit. As you walk to the trig point take note of the gate in the field boundary to your right. After enjoying the view to Dolaucothi and beyond, head back to this gate and into the next field.

Go left to walk downhill, keeping close to the hedge on your left. Look for a stile in the hedge ahead as you go. Climb over the stile and walk straight on to meet a track, where you go right. At a waymark post bear left to cross a meadow to a second waymarker (red trail). Head on to a gate next to a large oak tree, which opens into woodland.

Stay on this woodland path for about 500m to reach a gate that opens into a field. Head diagonally across the field to a stile. Cross the stile to arrive back on the track close to Dolaucothi Farm. From here, retrace your steps to the start.

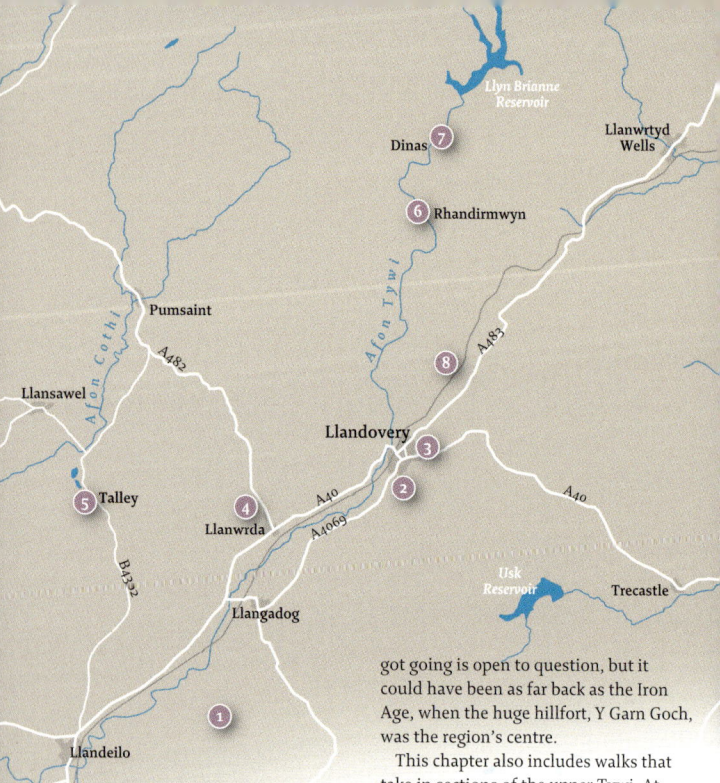

**Look out in Llandovery** for its statue of a drover. It's not a memorial to any one historical character but to generations of tough, resourceful cattlemen – Wales' very own cowboys.

The town was an important staging post for the cattle herds that were driven from the west to markets over the border in England. Quite when the droving trade got going is open to question, but it could have been as far back as the Iron Age, when the huge hillfort, Y Garn Goch, was the region's centre.

This chapter also includes walks that take in sections of the upper Tywi. At Dinas it is cold and crystal-clear as it tumbles between the boulders while at Rhandirmwyn it is a broader, shallower and altogether more sedate river that flows through ancient woodland.

A highlight in the east is the chance to enjoy a half-day walk along one of the country's best-loved railways, the Heart of Wales Line. One of the few branchlines to escape the 1960s' closure programme, it now has its own waymarked walking trail.

# East

1. **Y Garn Goch** 44
Children will love this relatively gentle walk to discover one of Wales' largest Iron Age forts

2. **In and around Llandovery** 46
Take your time on a tour of this riverside market town – there's 2000 years of history to discover

3. **Poor Man's Wood** 48
This woodland nature reserve is a joy all year round, but is at its best when bluebells are in bloom

4. **Llanwrda to Llansadwrn** 50
Majestic oaks mark field boundaries along the route of this gentle Tywi valley amble

5. **Talley Abbey** 52
The beauty of this abbey's setting is best appreciated as you ascend surrounding hills on this short but leg-testing route

6. **Rhandirmwyn** 54
The perfect walk for a hot summer's day with refreshment to be had along the way

7. **Dinas** 56
Discover a brigand's hideout and enjoy the peace of a classic Welsh oakwood on this upper Tywi adventure

8. **The Heart of Wales Line** 58
Take a picnic and take your time on this gentle cross-country yomp from station to station

# Y Garn Goch

**Distance** 3.2km **Time** 1 hour
**Terrain** moorland paths; steep in places
**Map** OS Explorer OL12 **Access** no public transport to the start

Carmarthenshire has lots and lots of Iron Age hillforts, but Y Garn Goch (The Red Cairn) is something special. It's the largest and arguably the most dramatic.

The hill actually has two forts. The smaller of the two encloses an area of 1.5ha (370 acres), while its much larger neighbour is a little more than 11ha (2760 acres). Today, Y Garn Goch (which is also known as Carn Goch) is usually quiet and attracts few visitors. That's quite a contrast to how it must have been 2500 years ago, when it was a busy tribal centre where hundreds of people lived and worked.

Start your exploration of the hill from the small public car park. Standing with the information board at your back, go straight ahead on an indistinct path that soon bears right.

The path passes a standing stone. It's of comparatively recent vintage – it was erected as a memorial to the politician Gwynfor Evans, the first Plaid Cymru MP.

Continue uphill towards Y Gaer Fach (The Little Fort). Take care as you go as the path is rocky and uneven. Bear left to make your way around the enclosure and head on towards Y Gaer Fawr (The Big Fort). The path drops down into the small valley between the forts. As you climb towards Y Gaer Fawr aim for the huge pile of loose stones ahead, which is part of the fort's rampart.

These stone defences are impressive today, but must have been a really

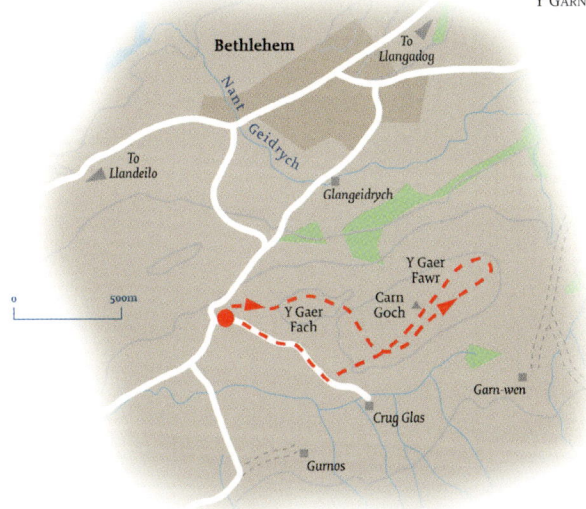

forbidding obstacle when they were constructed. They follow the natural contours of the hilltop, so were of varying heights; in places the stone-faced barrier would have been more than 10m tall. There's evidence that the fortifications were improved some time after 47AD, possibly as a reaction to the arrival in Britain of Roman forces. Within a few years the invaders headed west with Roman forces reaching the Tywi Valley by 70AD.

Bear to the right of the rampart to work your way around the fort. At a junction of paths go left through a gap in the rampart and into the fort's enclosure. Once inside you finally get a sense of just how big the fort is. The roughly rectangular enclosure is 700m long and 150m wide at its widest.

The only landmark among the heather, bilberry, cotton grass and rush is a small hillock topped by the loose stones of a burial cairn. It is thought to date from the Bronze Age and the fort may have been constructed to protect, or to celebrate, this spiritually-important location.

A path runs along the length of the enclosure and it is worth walking to the raised ground at the northeastern end, where the views of the Tywi Valley and Black Mountain are excellent.

Begin your return journey by retracing your steps to the gap in the rampart. Head on through and then carry straight on downhill, passing to the right of a small crag. When you come to a farm track, go right. It's then a short walk along the track back to your starting point at the car park.

◂ Looking east from the fort

# In and around Llandovery

**Distance** 3.7km **Time** 1 hour
**Terrain** town and country lanes, farmland paths **Map** OS Explorer 187 **Access** bus to Llandovery from Carmarthen

Carmarthenshire has so many beautiful churches and chapels that it would be hard to single one out as a favourite, but St Mary's Church at Llanfair ar y Bryn certainly deserves a place on the shortlist. Its tall gargoyle-ringed tower is a landmark, standing on a modest hilltop just beyond the town of Llandovery. Close to 2000 years ago a Roman fort stood on this hill; the church dates from the 12th century.

After exploring the churchyard, look for a stile and footpath fingerpost opposite the church gate. There's an impressive view from the stile to the north and west. From here start walking downhill, keeping close to the hedge on your left. Climb over the next stile and head straight on to reach and climb over a third.

Steps lead you up to the tracks of the Heart of Wales Line. Cross with care and walk down more steps to another stile. As you continue, keep to the left of a large ash tree to arrive at the next stile, which is by a stream. Walk on to a stile that you can see up ahead. Climb over this and go left to follow a path by a fence with a ditch on your right.

After crossing a footbridge, carry straight on to the final stile of this section of the route. Climb over this onto a road. Turn right and very shortly look for a footpath sign by a bridge on the left. Take this path to walk along a drive to a footbridge where you go left, passing through a kissing gate. Keep close to the wall on your right until you come to another kissing gate, which opens onto a tarmac drive. Go straight across this to a gate that opens into a field.

Walk on, keeping close to the fence on your right. Go through the next kissing gate you come to and bear right towards a shed. You'll soon see yet another kissing gate on the right, which opens onto a

## IN AND AROUND LLANDOVERY

◀ Llandovery's Market Hall

green lane. Go left and carry on to a gate and stile.

You will now be able to see the roadbridge that takes the A40 over the Tywi. Aim for this, going through a kissing gate close to the riverbank. When you arrive below the bridge itself you'll see that there are, in fact, two bridges – the roadbridge and, nearer to you, a footbridge. Take the narrow path that passes between the bridges. This brings you to the pavement beside the A40. Walk on into town, crossing to the far side of the road after going over the railway tracks.

Head straight on at the junction with Railway Terrace to continue along the A40, passing Llandovery College as you go. Stay on the main road, crossing its junction with Dingat View. At the next junction (with Broad Street), the A40 bears left. Follow it past the entrance to the livestock market and walk on until you come to the Castle Hotel.

Go right here to enter Llandovery's main car park. Look out for a statue of a drover on the left. Llandovery was an important centre in the days before the railways when large herds of Welsh beef cattle were walked to markets in England in the care of drovers.

Ahead you'll see Llandovery Castle and a second statue nearby. The first castle was built in the 1100s by a Norman baron and for the next four centuries was fought over by Anglo-Norman warlords and Welsh princes. It was attacked by Welsh forces in 1403 during Owain Glyndwr's national rebellion. The imposing, faceless statue that stands below the castle keep is a memorial to a local hero, Llywelyn ap Gruffydd Fychan, who was hung, drawn and quartered for supporting Glyndwr.

When you're ready to head on, bear right (with your back to the statue) to walk to the end of Castle Street, a narrow lane of cottages. At the main road, cross to Stone Street and follow this for 400m until you reach the A483 Llanfair Road. Go right, and continue past the town hospital. Take the second turning on the left after the hospital – it's then a 250m walk back to St Mary's.

47

# Poor Man's Wood

Distance 3.5km Time 1 hour
Terrain woodland paths, steep in places
Map OS Explorer 187 Access bus to
Llandovery, then a 10-minute walk

In a county that's blessed with plenty of beautiful woodland, Poor Man's Wood stands out. It's a marvellous mix of oak and hazel that is at its best in May, when the show of bluebells is breathtaking. In spring and early summer it is alive with song as migrant birds return to Wales for their breeding season. Look out for the pied flycatcher, a smart little black and white songbird, and the wood warbler, which sings its heart out from the treetops.

These days Poor Man's Wood is a nature reserve which is leased by the local Wildlife Trust, but it is owned by the town of Llandovery; it was left to the poor people of the town by their vicar, Rhys Pritchard, known as Yr Hen Ficer, 'The Old Vicar', on his death in the 1640s. Vicar Pritchard's will stipulated that townspeople could gather firewood for free, but only if they came and went on foot and carried what they collected on their backs.

This walk begins at the roadside on the A40. There's room to park two or three cars at the point where a track to Dan-yr-allt farm leaves the main road, by a large Wildlife Trust sign. (Alternatively, park at the castle car park, bearing east on the A40 for around 1km.) Head away from the road along the track which, after about 500m, comes to a farm.

Carry straight on, keeping the farm buildings on your left. Shortly after passing the last building you will see a path on the left, signposted 'Woods'. It skirts the bottom edge of the wood with the tree-covered slope on your right and open fields to the left. In time you come

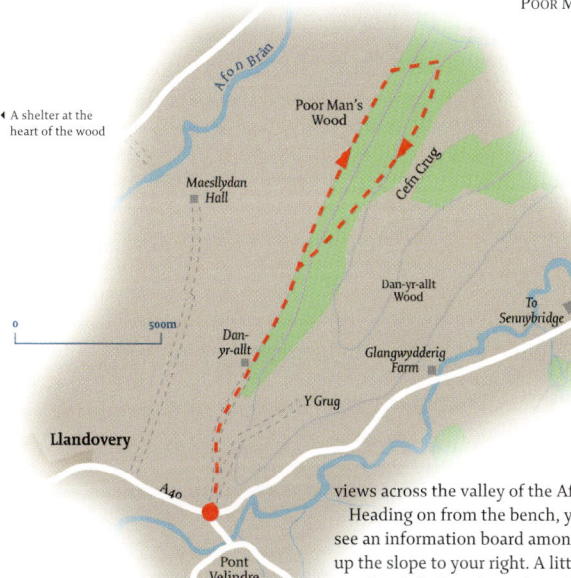

◂ A shelter at the heart of the wood

views across the valley of the Afon Brân.

to a grand, rustic kissing gate, which opens into the nature reserve. Go through the gate and keep left to head on along the public path.

This soon brings you to a small circular hut with tables and benches – the perfect spot for a picnic. From the hut, walk on a short way to a waymark post at the junction of two paths. Go right on the path that climbs up through the woodland. It's a long, steep climb and you'll be grateful for a moment's rest when you reach a bench two-thirds of the way up the hillside. In summer it's a good location for flycatcher-spotting, while in winter when the trees are bare there are

Heading on from the bench, you'll soon see an information board among the trees up the slope to your right. A little further on, shortly before the path reaches a footbridge, look for a waymark post. Turn sharp right at the waymark post on a narrow path that climbs uphill towards the information board that you spotted earlier. The path passes near the information board, but you'll need to make a short detour to get to it. It's there to mark one of the reserve's rarities – wild service trees. They are to the right of the board when you're facing it, protected in a fenced compound.

Go back to the path, which continues south, taking you through the wood on a gentle descent. In time, the path drops more sharply before returning to the reserve entry gate. From here, retrace your steps to your starting point.

# Llanwrda to Llansadwrn

**Distance** 5.5km **Time** 1 hour 30
**Terrain** farm tracks and roads
**Map** OS Explorer OL12 **Access** bus to Llanwrda; the village also has a stop on the Heart of Wales Line

**This short walk takes you between two neighbouring villages, Llanwrda and Llansadwrn. The former is, like many Tywi Valley communities, close to the river, whereas Llansadwrn sits on a small hill with great views.**

Start your walk in Llanwrda, just off the busy A40. Llanwrda stands at what was the junction of two 19th-century turnpike roads – now the A40 and A482. These days the A40 bypasses the village, and this walk starts out from the small bridge of the Afon Dulais on the line of the old road. If you're arriving by car there's on-street parking nearby and the village's bus stop is a little further along the route.

From the bridge, cross the A482 and carry straight on down the road opposite, past the village shop. You will soon pass the pub and then the bus stop. Shortly after the bus stop, look for a track, or green lane, on the right, which is signposted as being 'unsuitable for vehicles'. Take this lane, which is stony in places. It soon has you climbing away from the village between hedgerows and big oak trees. After around half an hour the track forks at a property called Ffynnon Garreg; keep left to continue heading uphill towards Llansadwrn.

When you come to a T-junction turn right to walk along the village street, which follows the curve in the wall that surrounds the churchyard. The church, which is dedicated to St Sadwrn, is at the heart of the village and stands at the centre of a large circular churchyard; many of the oldest churches in Wales have this design feature.

# LLANWRDA TO LLANSADWRN

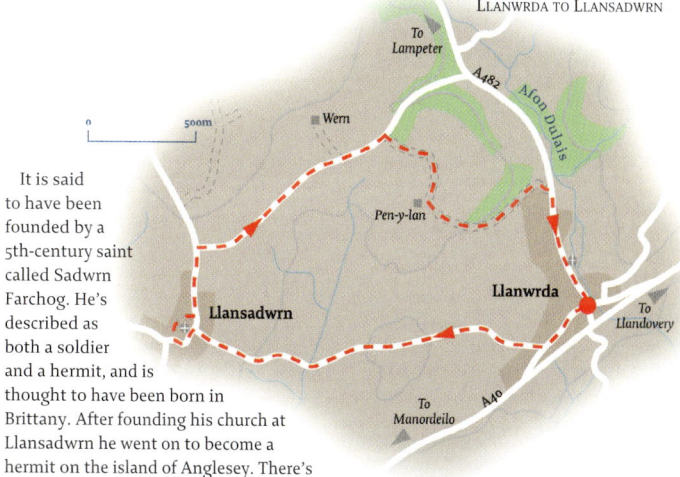

It is said to have been founded by a 5th-century saint called Sadwrn Farchog. He's described as both a soldier and a hermit, and is thought to have been born in Brittany. After founding his church at Llansadwrn he went on to become a hermit on the island of Anglesey. There's another Llansadwrn on Anglesey.

The church is a tangible connection with Sadwrn, but there's now nothing to show for Llansadwrn's most famous son. Rhys ap Gruffydd was born in the parish in the 1280s and went on to be one of the most influential men in Wales. But he is now best remembered as the captain of the Welsh contingent at the Battle of Crecy in 1346, where King Edward III's forces defeated a French army that was at least twice the size.

Following the line of the churchyard wall you approach a stone house. Before you reach it, go left on a track to continue walking around the churchyard. Where the track passes the Ebenezer Chapel (now a home) it becomes a narrow path.

Head on to pass the churchyard gate and bus shelter. It is worth taking a minute or two to explore the church, which is thought to partly date back to the 13th century. The porch is one of the oldest parts of the building.

Pass the bus shelter and go left to continue your circumnavigation of the churchyard. As you go there are great views on your right across the Tywi Valley to the hills to the southeast.

After going past the village pub and reading room, the route soon leaves the village and, in five minutes or so, comes to a junction. Bear right here and walk on for 1km until you come to a minor road on the right, which is close to a wood.

Turn right to walk along the narrow road, which brings you to a farm called Pen-y-lan. Stay on the road that goes into the farmyard and then bears left. Walk away from the farm on the road, which drops into the Dulais Valley. When the road brings you to the A482, turn right to walk through Llanwrda to your starting point at the bridge.

◂ Mature oaks to the south of Llansadwrn

# Talley Abbey

**Distance** 4km **Time** 1 hour 15
**Terrain** footpaths, woodland tracks; steep in places **Map** OS Explorer 186
**Access** bus to Talley from Carmarthen and Llandeilo

It's hard not to be impressed by the quiet beauty of the setting of Talley Abbey. The surrounding hills cup the ruins, which overlook a nearby lake. What the first occupants of the abbey thought of the location when it was founded 900 years ago is, sadly, not recorded.

Talley Abbey was a little different to others in the west of Wales. Its occupants weren't monks, but canons of the Premonstratensian order. The order's headquarters was far away in the north of France, at Prémontré. The group who took up residence at Talley were on a mission to extend the order's influence. They came at the invitation of the great Welsh prince, Lord Rhys of Deheubarth. Unlike the monks of other orders, the Premonstratensian white canons were more outward-facing in the way they lived their lives, sometimes serving as priests in nearby parishes. But the canons of Talley seem not to have prospered. The politics of medieval Wales were complicated, and there was friction with the well-established Cistercians.

Your starting point for this walk is the parking area at the gate into the abbey ruins. If there isn't space, there's also a parking area a short way to the north, close to a public toilet block.

With your back to the abbey gate, turn left to walk through the village to a junction. Go right here. After about 200m you will come to a concrete track on the right, close to a terrace of cottages. Take this track, which climbs the hillside and soon takes you into woodland.

At a waymark post, take the right-hand fork to walk on to a second waymark post.

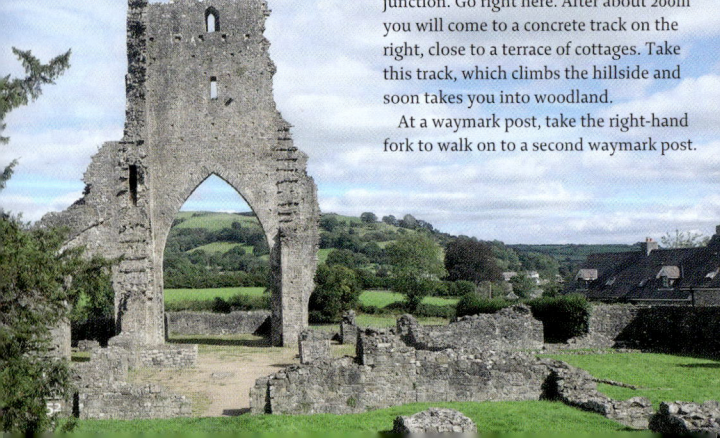

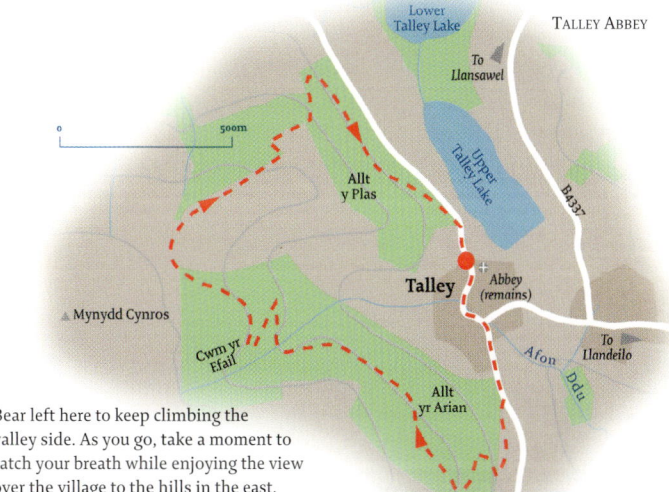

Bear left here to keep climbing the valley side. As you go, take a moment to catch your breath while enjoying the view over the village to the hills in the east.

At a field gate and waymark post, keep straight on to a picnic bench at a viewpoint. From this point onwards the route takes you through what was once Forestry Commission land but is now owned and run by a community group. The community association has marked out three walking routes through the woodland, each with its own colour-coded waymarking. There are yellow, red and blue routes.

From the picnic bench, take the forest track at the nearby waymark post to join the blue route. For the next 1.5km stay on the blue route (which is well waymarked), gaining about 100m in height to emerge on the flank of Mynydd Cynros. Go through double gates and straight on to another picnic bench with breathtaking views over the Cothi Valley. From this point the blue route begins its descent back to Talley.

In time you come to another viewpoint and a waymark post. Below are Talley's two lakes: Lower Talley Lake and, to the south, Upper Talley Lake. In between the two is a low man-made hill that is all that remains of Talley's castle.

Little is known about the castle's history, but it is thought that its centrepiece was a timber tower which occupied the mound's flat top. It is possible that it fell into disuse after the foundation of the abbey when territory that the castle controlled was transferred to the canons.

Go left to join the red route. The path takes you down a steep stretch of path to a second waymark post. Go right (red route) on a more gentle gradient and continue your steady descent until the path brings you to a minor road. Turn right to return to the church and abbey.

◀ The churchtower at Talley Abbey

# Rhandirmwyn

**Distance** 4.8km **Time** 1 hour 15
**Terrain** roads and footpaths
**Map** OS Explorer 187 **Access** no public transport to the start

The village of Rhandirmwyn comes as something of a surprise on a first visit. Approaching from Llandovery, the road twists and turns along narrow valleys before finally arriving at the Tywi, a wide open valley encircled by hills. At its heart lies Rhandirmwyn, once home to a thriving lead mining industry. At the time Carmarthenshire had a dozen lead mines, but the operation here was the biggest and most lucrative.

Mining is thought to have begun in Roman times, and it ended in the 1930s. By the early 19th century it was employing more than 100 men, while local farmers were involved too, working on contract to cart ore to the coast.

This route is a chance to combine a tour of the valley with a visit to both of its pubs, making it as much about refreshment as it is about walking. Along the way there's time to sit by the Tywi watching out for dippers and kingfishers.

Start out at The Royal Oak. With your back to the pub, go left and then bear right to take the narrow lane that heads downhill. The lane passes between hedgerows and some veteran oak trees. In time you will come to the village church, St Barnabas, which was built in Victorian times for the mine owner, Lord

Cawdor. One of his lordship's workings, Nant y Mwyn, was close by.

After passing the church, head on for 350m until you come to the Tywi. Cross the bridge and then look out for a waymark post and stile on your right. Climb over the stile and take the path along the riverbank and into woodland.

The path follows the line of the river through woods for 500m before bearing left. It's then a short, sharp climb with steps to a stile. Climb over the stile onto a quiet lane. Go right and continue for 1km until you come to the walk's second watering hole, The Towy Bridge Inn.

The pub has a small beer garden right on the river, which makes a nice place to spend time on a sunny day doing some fish-spotting. In late summer and autumn, salmon swim up the river to spawning grounds, while sewin (sea trout) do something similar in the early summer. Heading on, go over the bridge. Walk on for about 250m until you come to a junction where you turn right. Continue along the lane, which passes through woodland, before then offering beautiful views across the valley.

Many of the old lead workings were to the north of this stretch of road, and some of the cottages you pass along the way were once the homes of miners and their families. After about 2km you will come to The Royal Oak and the start.

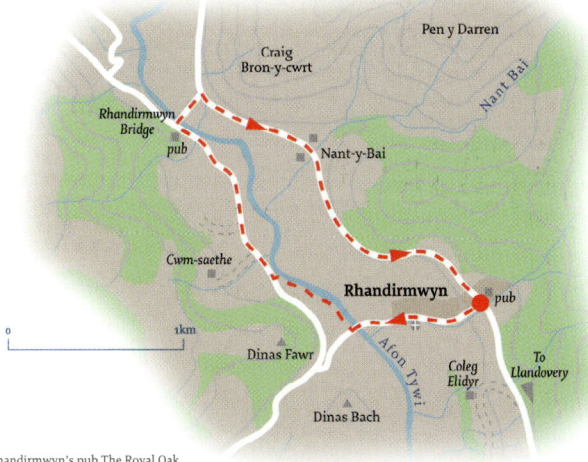

◂ Rhandirmwyn's pub The Royal Oak

# Dinas

**Distance** 6.4km (full route from dam), 3km (hill circuit only) **Time** 1 hour 30 (dam), 45 minutes (hill only)
**Terrain** roads and footpaths; steep and rocky in places **Map** OS Explorer 187
**Access** no public transport to the start

**The Tywi is the longest river to flow solely within the borders of Wales. From source to sea it covers a distance of 120km, mostly in a downhill rush.**

Since the early 1970s, the Tywi catches its breath at Llyn Brianne, the reservoir that lies at the point in the heart of Mid Wales where Carmarthenshire, Powys and Ceredigion meet. Here, Britain's highest dam holds back a huge volume of water so that the Tywi's flow can be regulated to supply homes further south.

This walk starts out at the dam before heading down the valley to explore Dinas, a beautiful wooded hill that stands above the confluence of the Tywi and its tributary, the Pysgotwr. An RSPB nature reserve, the hill is a perfect example of the sort of upland ancient oakwood that's now called Celtic rainforest.

Whether you choose to start your walk at the dam or at the RSPB's car park, take the minor road from Rhandirmwyn along the Tywi Valley towards Llyn Brianne (which is signposted).

You come to the RSPB car park entrance on the left shortly after passing the picturesque St Paulinus' Church. For the reservoir car park, head on past the RSPB car park entrance and take the second turning on the left, where there are two small flat-roofed buildings by the junction. It's then a short drive to the car park with great views over the reservoir's southern shore and the impressive dam.

From here, walk back the way you came to the RSPB car park. Cross this and enter

the reserve through the arch at the car park's southern end.

Walk along the boardwalk, which takes you across an area of meadow and on into the wood. The high rainfall levels in the valley create a perfect environment for ferns, mosses and liverworts. They grow in profusion on every surface, including the trunks and gnarled branches of the hill's oaks.

When you come to a waymark post, go right to leave the boardwalk and walk towards the river. Then head on along the path which, with plenty of ups and downs, takes you through the wood close to the river's edge. The Tywi is a magical river, which changes from season to season and day to day. In summer it is crystal-clear as it tumbles and turns between boulders.

In time you will come to a waymark post that offers two options: '55 mins walk' to the right or 'RSPB straight on'; take the latter. You are soon climbing wooden steps, which in time bring you to a more level stretch of path, before the path starts to rise again. It's quite a scramble in places until you eventually arrive at Twm's Cave.

The 16th-century outlaw Twm Sion Cati is often called the Welsh Robin Hood. He appears to have been more a confidence trickster than an armed robber, if there is any truth to the many stories told about his adventures.

Once you've caught your breath, and taken in the atmosphere of Twm's hideaway, retrace your steps to the waymark post and go left to continue around the hill. In time the path levels out and you're walking close to a meadow on your right.

When you come to a waymark post (marked '30 mins RSPB') go right to join a track that takes you to a field gate. It opens onto the valley road. Go left for a short walk back to the RSPB car park or a longer, more testing 2.5km uphill hike to the car park at the dam.

◀ The dam at Lynn Brianne

# The Heart of Wales Line

**Distance** 11km (one-way), 15km (with viaduct detour) **Time** 4 hours (one-way), 5 hours 30 (with viaduct detour) **Terrain** farm paths and minor roads **Map** OS Explorer 187 **Access** train to the start at Cynghordy from Llandovery

**The Heart of Wales Line offers one of Britain's most beautiful rail journeys, a cross-country adventure from Swansea to Shrewsbury with the added attraction of a long-distance trail which shadows the line's course across Mid Wales.**

The trail's logo features the line's best-known landmark, the 31m-high Cynghordy Viaduct. This route features a 10-minute train ride to Cynghordy, an optional detour to the viaduct and an excellent walk back to Llandovery.

On arriving in Cynghordy, walk away from the platform along the station approach to a junction at Cwmcuttan. It's left here for the viaduct, a 2km country lane hike each way; otherwise, turn right to head directly to Llandovery. At the next junction, go right again and pass through a tunnel under the railway line.

After 1km, as the road bends right, look for a waymarker on the left. Go through a gate and head on along a byway which becomes a tarmac road. At a junction, go left. When the road approaches a farm on the left, look for a waymarked gate on your right. Bear right to cross the field and a footbridge beyond, carrying straight on from here to a waymarked gate.

Go through the gate and on along the same line to cross another field and find a waymarked stile among trees (about 20m from the left-hand field corner). From the stile, walk straight across the flat field until it begins to slope uphill, then bear left to a stile. Climb this and walk on, keeping close to the hedge on your right. Go through a gate and bear left away from Rhandirberthog Farm along a stony track.

Stay on the lane to walk through Pantglas and on to a junction where you go left, and continue (with impressive views to the hills to the south and east) to

◀ Hills to the west of the Heart of Wales Line

reach a farm called Maes-y-gwandde.

After passing the farmhouse, go right on a concrete track. At a junction, keep left to walk on down into a valley. Stay on the track as it climbs again towards Cefnrickett Farm. As you near the farmyard the track swings right – look out for a waymarked gate on your left here. Go through this and bear right to walk along a hedgebank. At a waymark post, bear a little left across a field to a farm gate and small adjacent gate. Go through the small gate and straight on to a stile. Beyond this, continue with woodland to your right. At a junction, keep right to reach and climb over a stile. Go straight on to another stile on your left which takes you into a field – cross this and the track beyond to reach a small gate which opens onto a minor road. Turn left, then right at a junction towards the old Pont Dolauhirion over the Tywi.

Just before the bridge, go left to climb a waymarked stile. The gorse-lined route follows the course of the Twyi, passing through three kissing gates. Just after the third, bear right to follow the field boundary to another kissing gate opening onto a narrow path between bushes by a stream. Arriving at a gate onto a road, cross the road and a wooden footbridge, and carry on along the edge of a field, keeping close to a hedge, then a stone wall on your right. In time you come to a kissing gate that opens onto a drive. Cross to a second kissing gate and into a field, keeping the field boundary on your right.

Go through the next gate and aim for the shed ahead, looking out for a kissing gate as you approach. Go through this and turn left along a green lane to a stile and gate. Climb the stile and walk straight on with the hedge on your left. Pass through two kissing gates to soon meet the A40 where you go left to reach a level crossing and, just beyond, Llandovery Station.

The town of Llanelli, and the countryside around and about, played a significant part in Britain's Industrial Revolution. In the 19th century it was an industrial boom town, with steel and tin produced in huge quantities using coal mined close by.

So much high-quality tin was manufactured in the town that it was nicknamed 'Tinopolis'. Now, though, any signs of industry have all but gone, so as you walk along the nearby coast it's hard to imagine the smoke, dirt and noise.

The coastline of southern Carmarthenshire is a place of big landscapes. The tide rises and falls over huge areas of sand and mud, which are a feeding ground for wading birds and wildfowl. Wide open beaches are backed by sand dunes, which are sculpted by the tides and winter storms.

Heading west, the Tywi estuary is flanked by two castles – the nearest at Kidwelly on the Gwendraeth and, on the far side, Llansteffan. Water is a feature too as you venture inland to explore two very different lakes and climb to the trig point at the top of Mynydd Llangyndeyrn where, on a clear day, you'll have a sweeping overview of much of the county.

# South

**1** **Mynydd Llangyndeyrn** 62
Bag yourself a Marilyn in double-quick time on this short walk to what can feel like the top of the world

**2** **Kidwelly** 64
From the town's imposing Norman castle, venture off the beaten track into the surrounding hills and valleys

**3** **Kidwelly Quay** 66
History and nature converge in this coastal route with landmark quay, old coal-carrying canal and tidal sandbanks teeming with shorebirds

**4** **Llansteffan and Scott's Bay** 68
Discover a little gem of a beach, and get the chance to explore a castle too

**5** **Swiss Valley** 70
The picturesque Lliedi Reservoir is a highlight of this short walk through Llanelli's little slice of Switzerland

**6** **Tinopolis** 72
On a sunny day, the expanse of white sand can be dazzling on this beachside walk

**7** **Pembrey** 74
Take a saint's way to a viewpoint that looks out over a landscape with Spitfires and Hurricanes in its past

**8** **Llyn Llech Owain** 76
The slate-grey water of a lake that's been 10,000 years in the making is the focus of this route

# SOUTH

# Mynydd Llangyndeyrn

**Distance** 1.75km **Time** 45 minutes
**Terrain** footpaths, open heath, can be wet underfoot **Map** OS Explorer 178
**Access** bus from Llanelli and Carmarthen

Most people have heard of the Munros, the Scottish peaks that top 3000ft (914m), and the Munro 'baggers' who set out to climb all 282. Less well-known are the Marilyns – hills that stand 150m or more above surrounding summits. Marilyn-baggers have no fewer than 2011 summits to 'collect', including 158 in Wales. If you fancy having a go at bagging a Marilyn or two for yourself then Mynydd Llangyndeyrn is a great place to start.

At 262m above sea level, Mynydd Llangyndeyrn stands head and shoulders above south Carmarthenshire but is only a short walk from the nearest road. The views from the top are impressive, and it's a great location for a picnic.

Start your walk at the bus stop and shelter on the B4306 between Crwbin and Bancffosfelen, where there is space to park. The open commonland on both sides of the road here is Access Land, part of roughly one-fifth of Wales over which the public has a right of access on foot under the Countryside and Rights of Way Act of 2000.

Most of the Access Land at Mynydd Llangyndeyrn is to the east of the road, a crescent-shaped tract of heather, rock and rough grazing that is about 2km from end to end. It's a great place to spend time exploring, but for a short walk to bag your Marilyn start out by heading along the B4306 away from the bus stop in a northwesterly direction.

Cross the cattle grid and then go right at a waymark post to take a track that leads away from the road. Don't be put off by the 'private road' sign as the track is a public footpath.

Pass a covered reservoir on your left and

◄ A standing stone close to the summit of Mynydd Llangyndeyrn

walk on to a field gate. Go through the gate, pass the entrance to a farmyard and then bear right to a second field gate. Go through the gate and follow the hedgeline for about 100m before bearing right to climb towards the skyline. As you gain height you will see the trig point ahead, which marks the summit. Head straight for the concrete pillar.

The view from the top is vast. On a clear day look for Caldey Island, which is about 40km to the southwest. The common is designated as a Site of Special Scientific Interest (SSSI) because its underlying quartzite rock makes for a mosaic of dry heath, mire and bare stone. Curlews breed on the hill, as do grasshopper warblers. Look out in June and July for marsh fritillary butterflies.

From the trig point, carry on along the ridge as though you were heading to the sea. Ahead of you (but much, much closer) you'll see a telegraph pole. Just after you've passed this, bear left towards distant houses and, closer to you, a rocky crag. In time you'll see a tall standing stone, one of a number of prehistoric landmarks on the common. Aim for this, then pass by and carry on downhill on the same line.

Head towards a bungalow, looking out for a small gate as you go. The gate opens onto the private road that you used earlier. Turn left to rejoin the B4306, then left again to return to the bus stop.

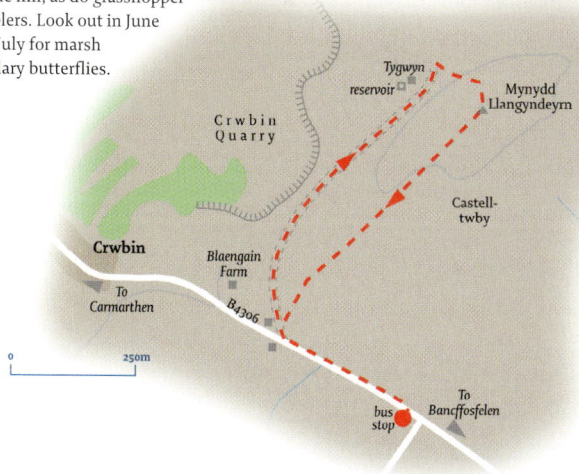

# Kidwelly

**Distance** 8.2km **Time** 2 hours
**Terrain** footpaths, farm tracks and roads
**Map** OS Explorer 177 **Access** Kidwelly is on the Carmarthen-Swansea railway line

This two-hour route takes you from close to Kidwelly's imposing castle and up into the hills to the north, where there are wonderful views to Carmarthen Bay and the Gower.

Start out in town from the bridge over the Gwendraeth. Take the riverside path at the northern end of the bridge, which passes below the castle's walls. In time the riverside path brings you to a kissing gate. Go through the gate to a street behind houses.

Walk straight on to Water Street, and turn right here. After about 300m, turn right again to walk along a narrow lane between tall hedges and reach a path on the left.

Take this path, which soon brings you to the Kidwelly bypass. Cross (with care) to a gate and footpath on the far side. When you reach Broadford Farm, go right to pass the farm. As you continue, look out for a sign on the left at Pwll Gwenllian, Gwenllian's Pool, which is worth taking a short detour to see.

Head on along the lane from the pool, crossing a stone bridge, then a metal one. At the next road junction, go left. Walk on for a little over 1km to meet a T-junction where you turn left. At the first bend in the road look for a stile on your left. Cross the stile and walk across a wide field towards trees. You will find a second stile and waymark post here.

Cross the stile and walk along a woodland path above the Gwendraeth. At a fingerpost, go right to cross a bridge over the Gwendraeth and

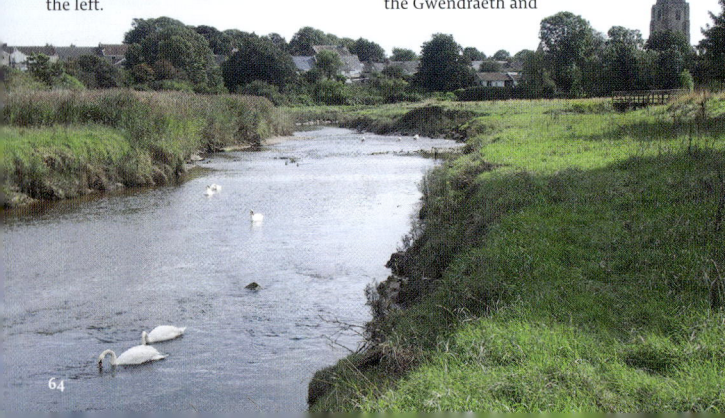

then bear left along a track leading to the A484. Turn left and follow the A484 for about 20m, then cross to a bridleway on the far side which climbs sharply from the road.

Look for a stile on the right. Cross this and take a path that in time enters woodland. Where the path leaves the wood follow it straight on, then bear left to a gap in a hedge. In the next field, the route climbs uphill towards trees where you bear right to follow the hedgeline.

Keep walking along the line of the hedge to buildings. Carry straight on to pass the farm and join its drive. A short way on you will come to a crossroads where bridleways meet. Go left; you will soon see the buildings of Penlan Uchaf ahead. The path bears left through the yard (look out for waymarkers).

Walk away from the farm on a tarmac lane. You'll soon come to a gate on the right. Go through this and walk straight on to a gate and stile. Climb over the stile and walk to the gate ahead, crossing a stream on the way. Beyond the gate, continue straight on to a line of oak trees on a rocky outcrop. Stay on the same line to a gate. Pass through this and head on through new woodland to another gate, which opens out onto a bridleway.

Walk on for around 600m. Where the bridleway bends to the left look for a waymarked gate on the right. Go through the gate and bear left to a second gate. Head on to the field gate opposite, and then cross the next field to yet another field gate. Go through this and keep close to the hedge on your left to find a path in the corner of the field. This takes you between houses back to Water Street. Turning right here, it's now a short walk back to your starting point.

◀ Kidwelly and the banks of the Afon Gwendraeth

# Kidwelly Quay

**Distance** 3.2km **Time** 45 minutes
**Terrain** footpaths **Map** OS Explorer 177
**Access** train to Kidwelly from Swansea and Carmarthen

This walk begins at the historic quay where from the 1700s coal was unloaded and shipped onwards from Kymer's Canal, which was built to carry the coal from pit to coast.

Business was good for the 18th-century entrepreneur Thomas Kymer. He had plenty of good Carmarthenshire coal to sell, and customers keen to buy. But he could only get a coal ship in and out on the highest of tides, which occurred just once a fortnight. It was a problem he solved in a unique way.

Kymer commissioned a canal to get coal to the coast and a quay at Kidwelly where each load could go from boat to ship. Completed in the 1760s, Kymer's canal and quay combination was the first in Wales. All these years later the quay remains a landmark, and a short stretch of the canal, which this route follows, survives too.

Start out from the large information board at the northern end of the quay's car park. Head to the end of the quay above the River Gwendraeth, where there's a great viewpoint.

Two arms of the Gwendraeth merge just beyond here. At its north end is the Gwendraeth Fach, while to the south is the Gwendraeth Fawr. A little to the west the Gwendraeth itself becomes part of something larger when it joins the Tywi. The confluence creates tidal sandbanks, mud and marsh that are home to thousands of shorebirds, especially during the winter months.

It makes this route ideal for a crisp winter's morning. Check tide times online and try to be at the quay an hour after high tide; as the water recedes, lapwing, redshank and curlew are among the birds that turn up to feed. When you're ready, continue on the path alongside the quay wall heading south (away from the

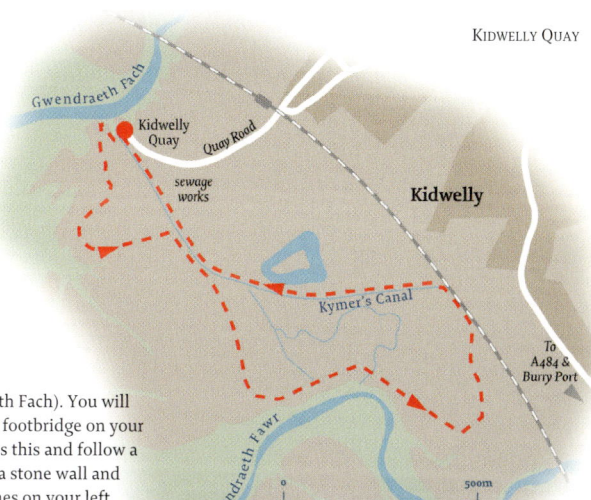

◀ Kidwelly

Gwendraeth Fach). You will soon see a footbridge on your right. Cross this and follow a path with a stone wall and gorse bushes on your left.

In time the path begins to rise as it nears Kymer's Canal and you will see a stone bridge ahead of you. Don't cross this bridge – instead go right to take a narrow footpath that leads between gorse bushes.

After about 150m you will come to two field gates, with a smaller gate in between. Go through the small gate and head on along the line of the hedge on your left. The path arcs to the left, taking you onto a bank and among small trees. When the path leaves the trees, stay on it, with a hedge on your left, to walk to a kissing gate.

Go through the gate and head on along an embankment that stands above the pasture on either side. For a time the bank runs arrow-straight, but then bears left – stay with it until it again changes course (going right).

Here, look for a kissing gate at the foot of the embankment to your left. Pass through the gate and walk on along the hedgeline to a track which rises towards a bridge over the coastal railway line.

As you near the bridge you will see a kissing gate on your left, which has a Coast Path waymark. Step through the gate and carry straight on along a path that runs parallel with the railway line. This brings you to a small metal gate. Go through this and walk on to a fork in the path by a bench. Take the right-hand branch. You are soon walking with the canal to your left.

Continue along the canal bank for close to 1km until you reach a road within sight of the quay car park. Go left. At the car park entrance, take the footpath on the left to return to the information board at the start of the route.

# Llansteffan and Scott's Bay

**Distance** 5.5km **Time** 1 hour 30 **Terrain** footpaths, farm tracks and minor roads **Map** OS Explorer 178 **Access** bus to Llansteffan from Carmarthen

**On a hilltop overlooking the confluence of the Rivers Tywi and Taf, the ruins of Llansteffan Castle are very picturesque. But the view from the castle is every bit as good; on a clear day you can see for miles in every direction. This coast walk ends with a detour to the castle – it's free to visit but it is worth checking opening times before you set out.**

The walk starts from the beach car park in the village of Llansteffan. From the corner of the car park furthest from the beach, pass an information board to take a narrow footpath that climbs away from the village.

When you come to a minor road, go left and later, where the road forks, bear right before going left at a waymark to join the Wales Coast Path, which passes through woodland. You'll soon walk past some steps (which drop down to the beach below), bearing right from the top of the steps to stay on the Coast Path. This takes you past a shelter and on around the headland towards Scott's Bay, a sheltered bay that can be a suntrap.

At a fork in the path keep left and walk on to the cove, where there's a single house, St Anthony's Cottage, set back above the beach. Go through a gate (with the cottage on your right) and cross a footbridge to continue on the Coast Path for about 1km, taking time to enjoy the views as you go.

Soon a gate opens onto open pasture.

Carry on along the Coast Path, which in time starts to lead away from the sea. After about 200m the path brings you to a gate that opens onto a minor road. Turn right to walk along the lane towards a farm called Lord's Park.

At the farm, keep the buildings on your right as you continue, heading towards Llansteffan Castle which you can see to the east. When you come to two field gates and a single stone gatepost, go through the left-hand one and carry on along the edge of the next field, staying close to the hedge.

Go through another field gate and drop downhill with the garden wall of St Anthony's Cottage on your left. When you come to the Coast Path go left to cross back over the footbridge below the cottage. On the far side of the bridge go left again to head inland, with the cottage garden on your left.

At a minor road, go right. In time you'll see the walled garden and parkland of Plas Llanstephan on your left. The mansion is now a hotel.

A little further on look out for a path on the right, which climbs to the castle and is well worth a detour. There was an Iron Age hillfort on the site long before the first Norman castle was built within its rampart. Llansteffan was a port in the Middle Ages, so was of strategic importance, and the castle was a flashpoint in the long conflict with acquisitive Anglo-Normans; it changed hands a number of times over the years.

When you've finished exploring the castle, retrace your steps to the road and head eastwards. The road soon brings you back to the point where you joined the Coast Path earlier; from there retrace your steps to the beach car park.

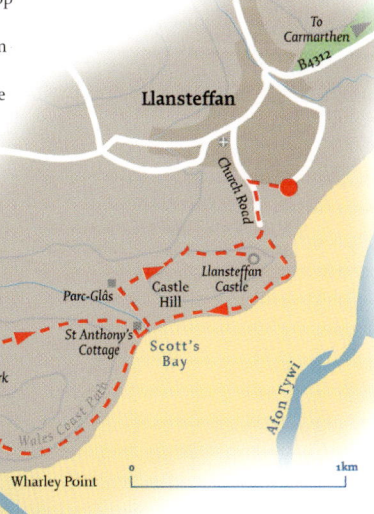

◀ Llansteffan Castle

# Swiss Valley

**Distance** 3.5km **Time** 1 hour
**Terrain** footpaths and roads
**Map** OS Explorer 178 **Access** bus to Swiss Valley from Ammanford and Llanelli

Quite how the Swiss Valley came by its name seems to have been lost in the mists of time. One theory is that it was the bright idea of an entrepreneurial Victorian faced with marketing new homes on the outskirts of Llanelli. Whatever the reason, the name sets apart what is an attractive area of countryside, and this short walk is a great introduction to Carmarthenshire's little bit of Switzerland.

Coming from the Cross Hands direction on the A476, look out for a large 'Swiss Valley' sign at the roadside and then take the next right-hand turn onto a minor road. This is the access road to the more southerly, and lower, of the two Lliedi Reservoirs.

That there are two reservoirs says something about the pace of Llanelli's growth during the 19th century. People moved to the town for work as it became a centre for steel and tinplate production, and they needed a reliable water supply. The lower reservoir was constructed in 1878, but the town continued to grow at such a rate that demand outstripped what one reservoir could supply, and a second Lliedi Reservoir was added in 1905.

This walk starts from the access road just off the A476. There's limited parking between the junction and the point at

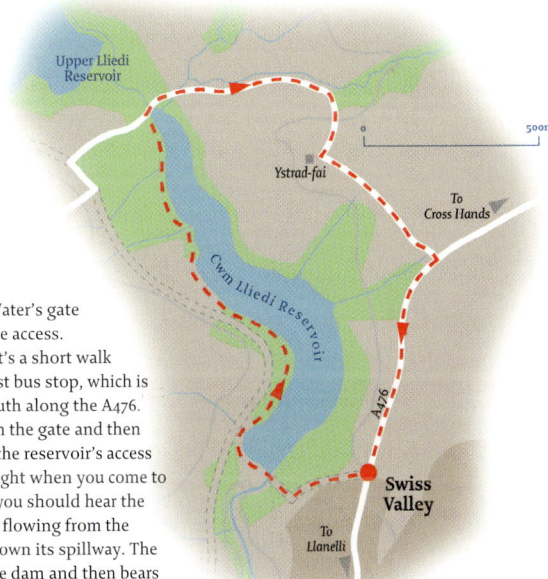

which Welsh Water's gate prevents vehicle access. Alternatively, it's a short walk from the nearest bus stop, which is 500m to the south along the A476.

Head through the gate and then walk on along the reservoir's access road, bearing right when you come to a house. Soon you should hear the sound of water flowing from the reservoir and down its spillway. The path crosses the dam and then bears right on a course that keeps close to the reservoir's western bank.

As you walk you pass through attractive mature woodland, which is home to dormice and rings with birdsong in spring. It is a mix of oak, holly, willow and alder. Look out too for the many very tall veteran Scots pines that are a feature of the wood. There are often anglers fishing along the western shore of the reservoir, a good place to catch brown trout, perch and rudd.

Non-human fish-hunters like the reservoir, too. If you can spare 10 minutes or so to sit quietly there's a good chance that you may see a heron or catch a glimpse of a passing kingfisher.

In time you pass the point at which the Lliedi enters the top end of the reservoir. Walk on until you arrive at a gate, which opens onto a minor road. Go right to cross a roadbridge, then right again at a junction.

After crossing a smaller second bridge, head on along the narrow lane, which climbs steeply out of the valley. When you come to a junction with the A476, go right. It's now a short walk back to Swiss Valley.

# Tinopolis

**Distance** 8.5km **Time** 2 hours
**Terrain** paths, mostly surfaced
**Map** OS Explorer 178 **Access** trains between Llanelli and Burry Port on the Swansea to Carmarthen mainline

The Carmarthenshire side of the Loughor Estuary was once a heavily-industrialised landscape where high-quality tinplate was made, earning it the nickname Tinopolis. But that soot-blackened past is long gone; where generations once did hard, heavy work, people now relax and enjoy seaside strolls. In the 1990s, many acres of post-industrial 'brown' land became what is now the Millennium Coastal Park. It's a 22km-strip of coast re-made for recreation and wildlife.

This route takes in part of the park, from North Dock, Llanelli, to Burry Port. You will be walking the Wales Coast Path for most of that distance, so look out for the path's seashell symbol on waymarks. It's a great location for a family outing. The path is level, which makes it particularly good for novice cyclists.

Start from the landmark building of the St Elli's Bay Bistro and Brasserie, close to Llanelli's North Dock. From here, walk west along the promenade or, if you prefer, along the beach.

During the winter months, it's worth timing your visit so that you're walking just after high tide. As water begins to flood out of the estuary, shorebirds fly in to feed in mud as it is exposed to the air; look out for oystercatchers and redshank.

After a little over 1.5km, bear right on rising ground to take the pink-surfaced path away from the prom. The coastal railway line runs in a tunnel below the small hill here, so there's a good chance that you will see trains heading west towards Carmarthen or east to Llanelli.

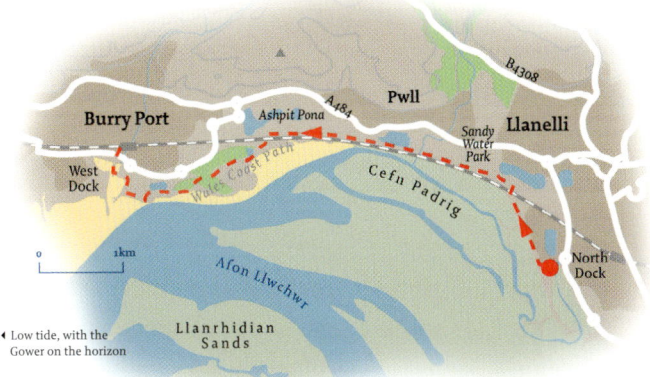

◂ Low tide, with the Gower on the horizon

Soon after, the path passes a large body of open water on your right, which is Sandy Water Park. Here you are close to the heart of what was Llanelli Steel Works, the largest iron and steel works in the world when it opened. That was in 1907 – it closed in 1981.

In the 19th century Llanelli was famous for its metal-working. It was known as Tinopolis in recognition of its reputation for tinplate manufacturing.

Stay on the Coast Path heading through the park until you pass a pavilion and playing field at Pwll. Close by you will come to a footbridge. Cross the bridge and then keep left to leave the tarmac path and head on along a narrower, rougher section of the route.

After around 1.5km, the route brings you to a broader tarmac path at a point that overlooks Ashpits Pond Nature Reserve. There, go left to cross a railway bridge and walk on along the waymarked Coast Path.

This eventually bring you to a slipway where the path swings to the right to pass Burry Port's lifeboat station.

Walk on along the harbourside path to bear left to a footbridge. Cross the bridge and then go right towards Burry Port. You soon come to the B4311 at a roundabout.

Cross the road and head straight on to a roadbridge over the railway. On the far side go right onto Station Road to the railway station.

Trains back to Llanelli take just a few minutes. If you arrived there by car, leave Llanelli Station and turn right to walk along Great Western Crescent, then right again onto Station Road. On the far side of the railway bridge, take the first turning on the right – this is Copperworks Road which later becomes Marine Street – and follow this for about 700m to reach a roundabout. Cross straight over this and then the bridge over the River Lliedi to return to the start.

SOUTH

# Pembrey

**Distance** 5km **Time** 1 hour 30
**Terrain** woodland paths and roads
**Map** OS Explorer 178 **Access** bus to
Pembrey from Carmarthen and Llanelli

**You get a better sense of the lie of the land around Pembrey by doing a bit of climbing. From above Court Wood, you can take in the low-lying land for miles around.**

It was a focus for activity during the Second World War. Relatively remote and near-flat, it was just what the war effort required. Spitfires were based at RAF Pen-bre (now a racing circuit) for a time and were later replaced by Hurricanes. It was also the base for the all-Polish 316 'City of Warsaw' Squadron. Nearby was an armament factory, which produced explosives. The site, once a workplace for some 3000 people, is now Pembrey Country Park.

This walk starts at Penybedd Woodland, just off the A484. From the car park take the main track through woodland, which is part of St Illtyd's Walk, a pilgrim route from Pembrey to Margam, near Port Talbot, a distance of 103km. You may not have heard of St Illtyd, but he has a connection to two patron saints – David and Patrick. Both saints are said to have studied at Illtyd's college, which was not far from Margam.

In time the track brings you past a wooden bungalow and on to a field gate. Go through the adjacent kissing gate and follow the track as it bears right, leaving the woodland. As you near farm buildings look for a turning on the right at a waymark post. Take this minor road, which soon brings you to a level crossing on the Carmarthen to Llanelli railway line. Cross the line and go straight on to emerge at the A484.

Cross the road to a minor road and follow this, passing a cycle trail (a shortcut back to Pembrey), to find a kissing gate on your right which opens into Ffrwd Farm Mire Nature Reserve. Go through the gate and take a path which crosses the mire on a raised causeway. In time you will arrive at a minor road.

On the opposite side are some large metal gates with a kissing gate to one side. Go through the kissing gate and head up the drive towards a house that you can see at the edge of woodland on the hillside ahead. As you near the house, you'll see a waymark post on the right. Take this path to walk along the edge of the lawn and then go right again on a path that leads up into the wood, where there are steps and a gate.

Pass through the gate and head left to walk along the edge of the wood to a waymark post. This is where you part company with St Illtyd's Walk by going right. The steep path takes you further into the wood. As you continue, keep close to the barbed-wire fence on your left and walk to a kissing gate. After passing through the gate, bear to the right of the hedgerow ahead.

Walk along the hedgeline (with the hedge on your left) to the crest of the hill and on to the mobile phone mast nearby. Go through the kissing gate close to the mast and drop downhill to yet another kissing gate. This opens onto a minor road where you turn right, passing what remains of one of the area's oldest buildings, Court Farm. First recorded in a document from 1361, it was occupied until the late 1940s. Just as you pass Court Farm look for a waymarked footpath on the right which leads you to a residential street. Carry straight on to meet the A484.

At the main road, turn right to walk 100m to a junction where you go left (signposted, Pembrey Country Park). Cross a bridge over the railway, then carry straight on to return to the start.

◀ Looking over Pembrey and the Loughor Estuary

# Llyn Llech Owain

**Distance** 4.5km (shorter version 2km)
**Time** 1 hour 30 **Terrain** farm footpaths, minor roads **Map** OS Explorer 178
**Access** nearest bus stop is at Cefneithin, around 700m from the farm shop drive

**A good lake deserves a legend to match, and Llyn Llech Owain's links it to an intriguing Welsh hero.**

The Owain in question was a 14th-century soldier-adventurer who led his own mercenary 'Free Company', fighting in Spain, France and Switzerland. He sided with the French against England during the Hundred Years War. Although he was born in Surrey, where his father owned a manor, Owain Lawgoch (Owain of the Red Hand) believed he was the rightful Prince of Wales. It's said he was planning an invasion when he was assassinated in France in 1377 by an English spy.

Over time he has become a semi-mythic figure who features in a number of folk tales. The Llyn Llech Owain story has him being left in charge of a spring, which he capped at night with a slab of stone. One night he neglected to replace the cap and a torrent soon filled the valley below, creating Llyn Llech Owain – the Lake of Owain's Slab.

Of course, the lake was already very, very old in Owain's day. It formed at the end of the last ice age, so is more than 10,000 years old, and was once much larger – over thousands of years peat has formed around the edges, restricting the open water. It's a pleasure to visit at any time of year. In early summer waterlilies come into bloom, while later dragonflies and damselflies enjoy the sun around the lake's margins. In winter, the lake and surrounding bog attract interesting birds. If you're lucky you may spot a little grebe or a snipe.

# LLYN LLECH OWAIN

For the shorter version of this route, head straight for the Llyn Llech Owain Country Park car park. For a longer walk that takes you through rough grazing that is great for wildlife spotting, start at the end of the Cwmcerrig Farm Shop drive, where it leaves the Gorslas-Cefneithin road (or use the farm shop and restaurant, and leave your car in the car park while you're exploring).

Walk along the drive, passing the farm shop car park's entrance and look for a footpath marker and small gate. Go through the gate and head on along the woodland edge, with the garden centre perimeter fence on your left. When you come to a gate on your left, step through and bear right to continue along the field boundary. Pass through a field gate and climb a gentle slope to reach a kissing gate. Go through the gate to soon arrive at a stile. Cross the stile into rough, rushy pasture and then follow the line of the boundary hedge on your right (and telephone lines overhead). In time you will see a metal kissing gate.

Pass through the gate and walk on to a second gate, which opens onto a minor road. Go right to walk a short distance to the country park entrance on the left. Walk along the drive to the park's car park. Go right here to pass a café and head on through woodland, following pink marker posts. At a junction, go left to take the path towards the Discovery Tower – the distinctive building at the lake's edge. When you get to the tower it's worth going up to the first floor, where there are excellent views over the lake and surrounding countryside.

Leaving the tower, go right to take the path that keeps close to the lake shore. Head on to circumnavigate the lake and, in time, return to the car park. From there, retrace your steps to your starting point at Cwmcerrig.

◀ The view over Llyn Llech Owain to the Discovery Tower

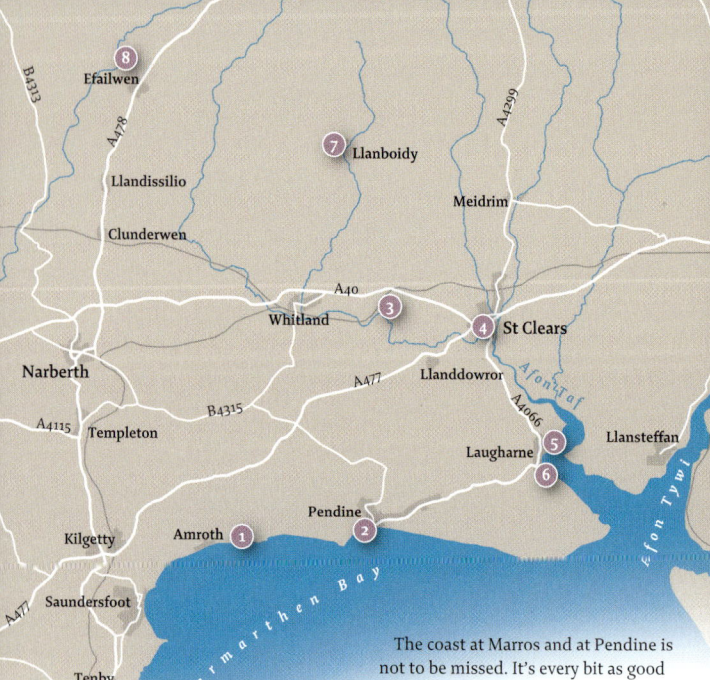

**Carmarthenshire has impressive castles** and handsome mansions, but arguably its best-known building is much more modest. Fans of the poet Dylan Thomas travel from around the world to visit his one-time home, The Boathouse, a waterside cottage at Laugharne.

Even if you don't know (or like) his poetry, you'll love the little town that he called home. If you can, spend a day exploring the town and surrounding coast and countryside.

The coast at Marros and at Pendine is not to be missed. It's every bit as good as what you'll find across the border in Pembrokeshire, but without the summer crowds.

At low tide Pendine's beach seems impossibly large. Take your dog; there's so much space, it's enough to make even the most level-headed canine go a little crazy. Head inland, too, to explore what was once border country, the medieval 'Landsker' that divided native Welsh from incoming Normans and Flemings. At St Clears and Llanboidy you can see the remains of the earth-and-wood strongholds that the newcomers built to dominate newly-won territory.

Laugharne Castle ▶

# West

1. **Amroth to Marros** — 80
   Get to know what is arguably the very best section of Carmarthenshire's beautiful coast

2. **Pendine** — 82
   Take it slow on this exploration of a seaside village that is world-famous for setting a much faster pace

3. **Whitland** — 84
   Dive into the hills to find the ruins of an abbey that was once a centre of power

4. **St Clears and Trefenty** — 86
   There's a hidden, bypassed feel to this triangle of country that sits between two rivers

5. **Laugharne and The Boathouse** — 88
   Take in the view that inspired Dylan Thomas before exploring the little town he loved

6. **Laugharne and Sir John's Hill** — 90
   Head up into the woods as you follow in the poet's footsteps on his favourite walk

7. **Llanboidy border country** — 92
   A varied walk that takes you through woods and along lanes in what was once disputed territory

8. **Efailwen** — 94
   With hills as a backdrop, you'll weave between counties on this exploration of Carmarthenshire's borderland

 WEST

# Amroth to Marros

**Distance** 6km (one-way) **Time** 2 hours 15 (one-way) **Terrain** coast path with some steep stretches, roads and footpaths **Map** OS Explorer 177 **Access** bus to Amroth from Tenby and Pendine, and from Marros back to the start

It's hard to imagine today, but this section of the Carmarthen Bay coast was once a centre of industry. Both coal and iron ore were mined in the area and shipped out using boats that were loaded on the beaches. You have to leave Carmarthenshire for this first-rate coastal walk – but only just. Amroth is in Pembrokeshire by about 2km.

On clear days there are good views to the Gower from Amroth's beach. If you're there on one of the year's lowest tides you may also see the stumps of trees that once stood in a forest swamped when sea levels rose at the end of the last ice age.

If you are arriving by car use the free car park behind the seafront shops. A path takes you to the front and the starting point for this route. This walk uses the Pendine-Amroth bus for the return from Marros. It's a journey of no more than 10 minutes, but there are only a few buses each day so it pays to plan ahead.

Start out by walking east along Amroth's seafront road. Pass Amroth Castle and keep on along the coast road to the end of the seafront, where you'll see a stone that marks the starting point of the Pembrokeshire Coast Path which you follow. The road climbs out of the hamlet of Water's Edge. Walk on to cross a bridge and enter Carmarthenshire. As you go, look for the Wales Coast Path shell symbol on a gate on your right beside the drive to a house called Merryfields.

Go through the gate and head on along the Coast Path, which passes between

◀ Above the beach at Marros

clifftop bracken and gorse. Stay on the Coast Path to cross a north-south path at a waymark post as you go.

In summer, it's worth taking regular halts as you walk as you're more likely to spot some of the many species of butterfly that thrive on this south-facing slope. They include the skipper and the speckled wood.

In time the path takes you through a wood of stunted oaks before dropping down to a footbridge. Cross the bridge and begin another long climb; this stretch of the path can feel like riding a rollercoaster. When you come to a bench sheltered by an arch-shaped tree take a well-earned rest and look back the way you've come. You should be able to make out Caldey Island, as well as the spire of Tenby's St Mary's Church.

As you continue eastwards along the Coast Path you're walking along the slope of Marros Beacon. Drop downhill to reach a gate, which opens onto the track to a property called Underhill. Go through the gate and turn left to leave the Coast Path and head inland. Stay on this unsurfaced road for 20 minutes or so until you arrive at St Lawrence's Church, Marros.

The church has a fine example of the tall crenellated towers that are a feature of south Pembrokeshire and west Carmarthenshire. Built by Norman colonists in the 1200s and 1300s, these towers served a practical purpose. In times of trouble, locals could use their church like a mini-castle.

The stop for your bus back to Amroth is just across the road from St Lawrence's. While you wait take a look around the churchyard. On the outside of the churchyard walls you can make out carved graffiti, some of which is close to 250 years old. It's thought to be the initials of the parishioners who contributed to the wall construction project.

# Pendine

**Distance** 3km **Time** 1 hour
**Terrain** footpaths, woodland paths, roads
**Map** OS Explorer 177 **Access** bus to
Pendine from Tenby and Carmarthen

**For a few years, almost a century ago, the name Pendine was known around the world. At the time the seaside village was the setting for a duel between two racing drivers over who could claim to be the world's fastest.**

To get a sense of what made Pendine suitable for the battle you need to head to the southern end of the seafront, where this walk begins by the public toilet block. Pass the café next door to reach steps that begin to climb the cliffs of Dolwen Point. It's quite a climb with lots of steps along the way, so pause to look back and take in the full length of Pendine Beach, which was so important for those time trials.

To make a bid for the land speed record, the 1920s drivers had to complete a timed mile. But it took a while to get up to top speed and, when the mile was covered, to decelerate; in all, around 8km of smooth, firm sand was called for. Pendine Sands offered that, with space to spare. From end to end the beach is about 11km long.

The first Pendine record was set by Malcolm Campbell in 1924 when his car *Bluebird* travelled at a shade above 146mph. He returned in 1926 when he managed to break the 150mph barrier.

At his first attempt, John Godfrey 'JG' Parry-Thomas smashed Campbell's record, driving his car *Babs* at 171mph. Campbell responded in February 1927,

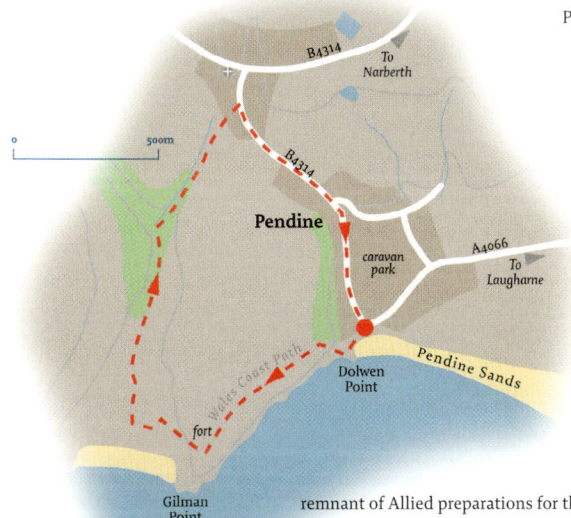

when he achieved more than 174mph.

Within weeks Parry-Thomas was back. However, as *Babs* reached around 170mph something went catastrophically wrong, and he died in the subsequent crash.

Head on along the Coast Path to reach a craggy summit above Gilman Point, where you look to a sheltered cove called Morfa Bychan. Beyond it, you should be able to see Tenby – as the gull flies, it's about 11km away.

The path drops down to a gate at a waymark post where the route goes right to take a track heading inland. It's worth taking a break at this point to spend some time on the beach. Little Morfa Bychan is quite a contrast to its neighbour, Pendine. Look out for slabs and chunks of old masonry among the pebbles, which are a remnant of Allied preparations for the D-Day Landings of 1944. A stretch of seawall was built at Morfa Bychan as a replica of German defences in Normandy. Troops then practised blowing up sections of the wall to create gaps big enough for tanks to drive through.

From the beach, head inland on the stony track that climbs the steep valley behind the beach. After a time you'll hear fast-flowing water where a stream drops into a culvert. A little further on you will come to a bridleway waymark. Go right here to follow a narrow uphill path through woodland.

Where this path joins a second farm track, bear right to carry on uphill to the older part of Pendine, which focuses on St Margaret's Church. At the road, which is the B4314, turn right to walk downhill to the seaside part of the village and the route's starting point.

# Whitland

**Distance** 5.6km **Time** 1 hour 15
**Terrain** farm tracks, roads and paths
**Map** OS Explorer 177 **Access** trains to Whitland from Carmarthen

Bypassed by the busy A40, the little town of Whitland is missed by many visitors to West Wales, but it's definitely worth taking time to explore. This pleasant walk takes you through the countryside around the historic border town, and to the ruins of the ancient abbey that gave it a special significance in the complicated world of medieval Wales.

If you're arriving by car, park at the picnic area at St Mary's Church, close to the old bridge over the Taf. Then walk to town along the B4328, crossing the railway at the level crossing. Continue along what is now St John's Street to its junction with Market Street. Turn right and carry on, passing The Fishers Hotel. Soon after this pub, look out for a footpath waymark post on the left.

Take this path to walk along a row of modern houses to allotments. Head on along the track through the allotments to a kissing gate. Go through the gate, then walk on along the edge of a large field to a second kissing gate. Pass through the gate into another field and walk towards powerlines ahead.

Beyond the powerlines you'll see the A40, which at this point is raised on an embankment. As you near the road you'll see that there's an underpass through which the footpath leads. From the underpass go into the field beyond and bear right to a footbridge. Cross the bridge and walk across the pasture ahead on the same line, climbing uphill.

Over the brow of the hill walk on to a kissing gate next to a mature tree in the hedge ahead of you. Go through the gate and stay on the same line to cross the next field to a footbridge. Once you've crossed the bridge bear right to cross a final field to a kissing gate, which opens onto a quiet lane. There go left to walk to the hamlet at the site of Whitland Abbey.

◂ Whitland Abbey

What remains of the abbey buildings are on the left. Look for a signpost on the left, which indicates the gate to the ruins. A Cistercian house was founded near Carmarthen in 1140, but it was moved to Whitland 15 years later. There's not much to see now, but in its day Whitland was the mother house of Cistercian houses in Wales and Ireland. The abbey's patron was Lord Rhys, Prince of Deheubarth.

During his 40-year reign Rhys was in almost constant conflict with the English crown and had an especially vexed relationship with King Henry II. When Henry's invasion of Wales failed in 1165 the king took his anger out on hostages that he had taken, including Rhys' son Maredudd. Vengeful Henry had Maredudd blinded. Whitland has a connection with this harrowing story; on his return to Wales, Maredudd lived out his days as a Whitland monk.

Retrace your steps and look for a road sign that says 'Byway to Whitland'. Take this narrow byway which soon passes through a ford on the Afon Gronw (don't worry, there's also a footbridge, so you won't have to get your feet wet). Head on along the lane, bearing left when you come to a Y-junction. Eventually, the lane brings you to a road. Go left to shortly cross a bridge over the A40 and continue on into Whitland along North Road.

When you come to the end of North Road go left along Llangan Road and then take the first turning on the right, which is St John's Street. Retrace your steps to the station, or to St Mary's.

Just before you reach the level crossing it is worth making a short detour left along St Mary's Street to the Hywel Dda Centre, which remembers the 10th-century Welsh ruler. Hywel Dda, Hywel the Good, is said to have called lawyers together at Whitland to put together a book of laws that, for their time, were compassionate and full of common sense.

# 4 WEST

# St Clears and Trefenty

**Distance** 9km **Time** 2 hours 30
**Terrain** footpaths and farm tracks
**Map** OS Explorer 177 **Access** bus to
St Clears from Carmarthen

Today, the Carmarthen-Haverfordwest road bypasses St Clears, which means most travellers miss it. But the little town, and the low-lying landscape to the south, are definitely worth exploring. This walk takes you from the town's main car park through the old heart of St Clears and on to a ruined church said to have been used by pilgrims on their way west to St Davids.

From the car park in St Clears, go left to walk to a crossroads, then left again onto High Street (A4066). Cross a slip road and continue over a bridge above the A40. In time you'll come to the ornate lychgate of St Mary Magdalene's churchyard. With the nearby castle, it was at the heart of the walled Norman town.

Shortly after passing the lychgate turn left onto a narrow lane. It bears to the right, passing behind houses. At a fork in the path (the bramble-covered hill to the right was the castle), keep left to reach a road. Go left to cross the Afon Cynin, joining the Wales Coast Path.

Bear right, cross a cattle grid and walk on across a meadow. As you near a hedge, leave the track to walk to a metal gate on the left and go into the next field.

Head towards Pant-dwfn, the farm on the hill above you. Look for a field gate to your right. Go through this gate to a track and bear left here, passing footpath waymarkers as you continue.

Where the track leaves the farm you come to a fork; take the right-hand branch to carry on to a gate. Go through this gate and head straight on.

When you come to two field gates go through the one on the left. Walk on

◂ All that now remains of St Clears Castle

along the field edge, passing a gate in the hedge along the way (but not going through it) to arrive at a kissing gate.

Go through this and walk on across the field towards Foxhole, the farm you can see nearby. Pass through a gate close to a large tree and continue on the same course to reach gates on either side of the farm track.

Walk through both gates and, on your previous course, carry on to a kissing gate in a hedge. This is where you leave the Coast Path, going right after crossing a footbridge. You soon arrive at the main gate of the next farm, Trefenty. In the Middle Ages this was the home farm of a commote, or lordship, called Ystlwf, or Oysterlow. A little to the west of the house there's evidence of a simple castle. Walk on to Trefenty, passing the farmhouse and then going left to walk along the edge of the farmyard to a gate that opens onto a field.

Go through the gate and continue, passing to the right of the summit of a small hill. Walk to a field gate (and stile) that opens into the last cultivated field before the marshland beyond. Head on along the line of the hedge towards what looks like a small wood ahead, but is actually the grove of trees surrounding the walk's end point, St Michael's Church. A stile gives access to the churchyard. Abandoned in the 1840s, it had been a place of worship for at least seven centuries; its 12th-century font was relocated to a new church.

It's an eerie place. Look for some old gravestones to the south of the building. They're said to be pilgrims' graves, although there's nothing on record to back up that story. When it's time to go, simply retrace your steps to St Clears.

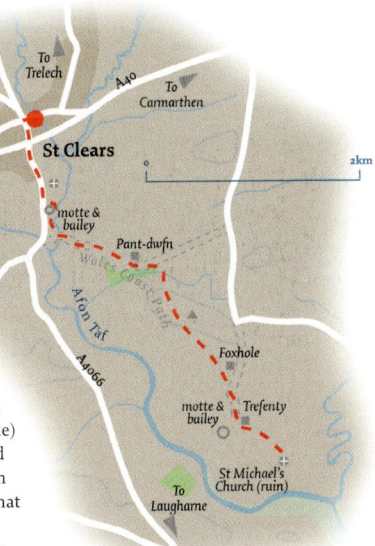

# Laugharne and The Boathouse

**Distance** 4.5km **Time** 1 hour 15
**Terrain** footpaths and quiet roads
**Map** OS Explorer 177 **Access** bus to
Laugharne from Carmarthen and Pendine

If you can name only one Welsh poet, it's almost certainly Dylan Thomas. The Swansea-born writer was already an international celebrity when he died in 1953 at the age of just 39.

These days his many devoted fans travel from around the world to West Wales to experience something of the sights and sounds that informed his writing. There are a number of locations on the Dylan homage tour, including two that lay claim to be the inspiration for his best-known work, the play for radio *Under Milk Wood*.

Thomas was born in Swansea, but had family links with both New Quay in Ceredigion and Laugharne on the Carmarthenshire coast. If you can, take time to read *Under Milk Wood* (or listen to the classic Richard Burton recording) before you visit Laugharne. If you do, you'll see the parallels between real world Laugharne and Llareggub.

Start out from the car park below Laugharne Castle. Cross the small bridge to follow the footpath that bears left between the castle and the Taf. At a fingerpost, the path splits – go left to climb towards the town. When you come to the first houses follow the lane to the left and then go right to walk to a junction. There go right to pass a graveyard and walk to the gates of Laugharne Park.

Turn right to walk on along a narrow road. There's a great view over the Taf and

you soon come to Dylan Thomas' writing shed. Between 1949 and 1953 the Thomas family lived at The Boathouse, perched above what the poet called 'the heron priested shore'. He converted the house's wooden garage to use as his study. It has been preserved as if he had just popped out for a pint at Brown's, his favourite pub. The path then passes above The Boathouse (which is an excellent little museum of all things Dylan Thomas) and takes you on into woods. When you come to a road, cross over and head straight on along the woodland path.

In time you will come to a kissing gate, which takes you into a field. Head on, keeping close to the fenceline above the Taf. Further on the path leads you into woodland once again. When you come to a footbridge, walk across and head towards the building on the far side of the field, which is Delacorse Farm.

At the farm, go through a kissing gate and pass to the left of the house, following Coast Path waymarkers to a track that heads uphill away from the farm. Stay on the track which climbs steadily until it joins a tarmac-surfaced lane where you go left.

Stay on the narrow lane for 500m until you come to St Martin's Church. There's a small kissing gate on the right that opens into the churchyard.

Soon after passing the kissing gate, the lane takes a sharp turn to the right. A little further on, go left at the bridleway waymarker. The gate that you pass on the right opens into the church's graveyard extension. If you'd like to pay your respects to the poet, take a moment to go in and explore; he shares a plot with his wife, Caitlin, and their grave is marked by a simple cross.

Stay on the bridleway, keeping right where a footpath joins from the left. The sunken lane then continues downhill to bring you out onto the road at the gate to Laugharne Park. From here, retrace your steps to the walk's starting point.

◀ The Boathouse stands close to the shore, overlooking the Taf

# Laugharne and Sir John's Hill

Distance **4.5km** Time **1 hour 15**
Terrain **minor roads and footpaths, steep in places** Map **OS Explorer 177**
Access **bus to Laugharne from Pendine and Carmarthen**

Dylan Thomas celebrated his 30th birthday – 27 October, 1944 – with a walk up out of Laugharne to Sir John's Hill, the wooded high ground to the south. The day is remembered in *Poem in October*. This walk mirrors his route on that morning. It then takes you along the coast and finally returns to the town.

As with the previous walk, the starting point is the town's main car park at the castle. Leave the car park at its southern end, furthest from the castle (look out for the carved-wood bust of Dylan Thomas as you go). Here, a tarmac road leads towards the wooded hillside.

The road soon ends, becoming a footpath: look out for a 'Dylan's Birthday Walk' sign. The path bears left, heading towards a low-level building. Shortly before you reach it you come to a waymark post where you should turn right to begin the climb up the wooded flank of Sir John's Hill.

As you climb you encounter viewpoints from which you can see the Taf, the bay and mile upon mile of saltmarsh. In time you will come to a fork in the path – take the path on the left to begin your descent.

Continue along the path as it reaches marsh-level, hugging the base of the hillslope and bearing west towards Salt House Farm. When you get close to the farm, look for a field gate and kissing gate on the left. Go through the kissing gate and carry on along the track, passing the farm and

# LAUGHARNE AND SIR JOHN'S HILL

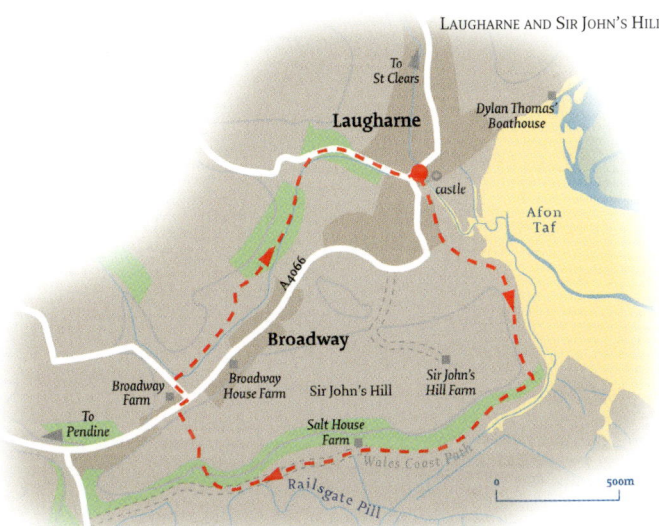

aiming for the quarry in the distance. In time you will come to a waymark post that indicates a stile on the right.

Climb over the stile and take the path that leads through the woodland. It's a tough climb, but eventually the path brings you to a pair of stiles at the woodland's edge. Climb over the first stile and then bear right to go over the second. Now turn left to walk along the line of a hedge. Stay close to the hedge as it crests the hill and drops into a valley. When you come to a stile, climb over and head on to a second stile by the side of the A4066.

Climb over onto the road (with care) and then cross to the far side and go right. Take the first turning off the main road on the left. Opposite the entrance to a caravan park you'll see a fingerpost that points the way to a footbridge and stile.

Climb over the stile and then walk along the next field, keeping close to the stream on your right.

You will soon come to a stile in a hedge. Don't climb over; instead go left to follow the line of the hedge until you come to a path in one corner of the field. Take this path which soon becomes narrow and has tall banks on both sides. When you come to a stile, climb over and head on, passing close to a house (on your right).

At a waymark post, keep left to walk on along a narrow lane. When you come to a junction stay left. At the next junction, go right to walk along a narrow road with a stream on your right. As you come to the edge of Laugharne, head straight on along the road to arrive at a square with a cross and, just a little further on, the castle and car park.

◀ A view to the southeast on the climb up Sir John's Hill

# Llanboidy border country

Distance 7km Time 2 hours
Terrain footpaths and quiet country lanes
Map OS Explorer 177 Access bus to
Llanboidy from Carmarthen

**This walk takes you through the attractive hilly countryside around the village of Llanboidy. Along the way you will be walking sections of the Landsker Borderlands Trail, a 96km long-distance path which explores landscapes that were once hotly contested.**

'Landsker' is an Old Norse word for divide and in recent times it's been used to describe the string of around 50 strongholds that once marked out a frontier across Pembrokeshire and into Carmarthenshire. They were built in the 12th century by the Normans and their Flemish allies to defend land taken from the native Welsh.

It's fascinating how, centuries later, there are still apparent cultural and linguistic differences on either side of this notional border. Roughly speaking, you are more likely to hear Welsh spoken north of the line than south of it. The contrast was greater in the 17th century, when the historian George Owen described the country south of the line as 'The Little England beyond Wales'. It's a description that you'll still occasionally hear today.

Llanboidy earns its place on the line because it had a castle or, to be more precise, a motte-and-bailey fort. These simple castles were little more than a circular ditch and an earth mound, with wooden walls.

Start your walk from the village car park. Opposite the car park entrance you can see a mound in the field across the road – that's all that remains of the Norman stronghold.

From the car park, go left to pass the public toilet block and head into the

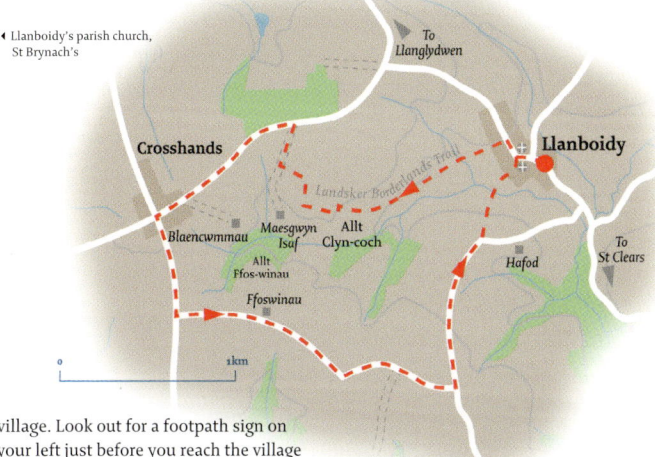

◀ Llanboidy's parish church, St Brynach's

village. Look out for a footpath sign on your left just before you reach the village school. Take this path, which is a narrow green lane. Where the lane ends, head on along the fenceline.

The footpath leads you uphill towards large trees ahead. As you get closer, look out for a stile and waymark in the corner of the field. Climb over the stile and continue straight on along a grassy track. In time you'll see another stile with a waymark on your right.

Cross the stile and bear left to the corner of the field. There, go right to walk uphill along the line of the hedge. Look out for a waymark on a fencepost and go left when you see it to meet yet another stile and field gate. Head into the next field and then bear right to walk along the boundary fence (passing a redundant stile as you go) to a stile that is close to a telegraph pole.

Climb over the stile and walk on to reach a concrete track where you turn right. It's now a short distance to a minor road where you turn left, enjoying views of the Preseli Hills to the west as you go. At a hamlet called Crosshands turn left at the crossroads. Stay on this lane, passing a farm called Ffoswinua along the way, to reach a T-junction. Turn left to begin the steady descent into the valley of Afon Gronw. About 1km further on you come to a junction where there is a green lane that's marked as unsuitable for vehicles.

Go left to walk along this lane which is, in parts, hemmed in by rocky banks festooned with ferns and mosses. The lane crosses the river at a small bridge and, soon after, you arrive back at Llanboidy. The lane joins the main street close to the post office. Turn right to walk back to your starting point.

# Efailwen

Distance **10km** Time **3 hours**
Terrain **footpaths, quiet roads**
Map **OS Explorer OL35** Access **bus to Efailwen from Narberth**

**Welcome to border country. On this route you'll spend time in both Carmarthenshire and Pembrokeshire, with the Preseli Hills as a backdrop.**

The walk's starting point is at the southern end of Efailwen, where there's a bus stop on the main A478 road. There's also on-street parking close by.

Little Efailwen has a claim to fame as the location of the first of the demonstrations that became known as the Rebecca Riots. There's a café in the village called Caffi Beca in honour of the locals who took part.

In the 1830s struggling local farmers felt that the road tolls they had to pay were an unfair tax. So, when new toll-gates were built at Efailwen in 1839, a crowd gathered and tore the gates down. The protest struck a chord and spread to other parts of South West Wales, continuing until 1844. In time there was a change in the laws governing main roads in Wales. The campaign would probably now be long forgotten if it wasn't for the fact that the protesters – mostly men – chose to wear women's clothes, and called themselves Merched Beca (Rebecca's Daughters). It's not clear why the name Rebecca was chosen. One theory is that it was a reference to a line in the Book of Genesis, which talks of 'blessed' Rebecca as 'the mother of thousands of millions'.

From the junction close to the bus stop take the road signposted 'Llangolman'. You will soon come to a track on the left, signposted 'Fferm Clyngwyn'.

Take this track, which heads west. At the farm walk straight on through the farmyard and continue westwards to the valley of the Eastern Cleddau.

The track zigzags downhill into the valley. Today it's peaceful, but it was once at the heart of the local slate quarrying industry. The green-grey slates were used

◀ Looking to Pembrokeshire's Preseli Hills

locally and much further afield.

In time you'll see an information board (about one of the quarries, Clyngwyn) ahead; shortly before you reach it, go left on a path into woodland. Stay on this path until you come to a waymark post.

Bear right here, passing some buildings, to the point at which the track reaches a minor road. Go right to pass Rhydwilym Chapel and cross a bridge over the Cleddau. Walk on uphill, heading straight on at the first road junction before then taking a footpath on the right.

Stay on this path through the wooded valley until you come to a stile that opens onto a field. Climb over the stile and head on, keeping close to the hedge and bank on your left. The track becomes a lane, which is muddy in places.

Carry on along the lane as it heads towards Pencraig-fawr. As it nears the farm, the track bears left and brings you to a field gate on your right. Go through the gate to the farm track, then go left. Walk along the track until you come to a minor road, then go right. Stay on the lane for about 1km, passing St Colman's Church along the way, to reach a junction.

At the junction, go right and walk on to reach the village of Llangolman. As you near the small green, look for a footpath sign (opposite the community information board) where you go right. The path then crosses a farmyard. Shortly after passing a barn, look out for a stile on the left. Cross the stile and walk to some waymarked steps in the wall on the far side. Climb over the wall and then head on along a path through woods.

You will soon come to a narrow footbridge over the Cleddau. Cross the river and stay on the path which passes another of the valley's disused quarries, Gilfach. At the quarry, go right to walk along a narrow path through woodland. When the path brings you to a track, go left to pass Gilfach Cottage and, later on, Gilfach-ddofn Farm. At the farm drive, go left to walk to a minor road.

At the road, turn right. Then, stay on this road for about 2km to return to your starting point.

# Index

| | | | |
|---|---|---|---|
| Aberglasney | 18 | Llangathen | 18 |
| Abergorlech | 38 | Llansadwrn | 50 |
| Amroth | 80 | Llansteffan | 68 |
| Beacons Way | 20 | Llanwrda | 50 |
| Bethlehem | 44 | Llyn Brianne | 56 |
| Boathouse, The | 88 | Llyn Llech Owain | 76 |
| Brechfa Forest | 36 | Marros | 80 |
| Bronwydd | 12 | Merlin's Hill | 10 |
| Burry Port | 72 | Mynydd Llangyndeyrn | 62 |
| Carmarthen | 8 | Nant Esgair | 32 |
| Carreg Cennen | 20 | National Woollen Museum | 32 |
| Cefneithin | 76 | Newcastle Emlyn | 26 |
| Cenarth | 26 | Paxton's Tower | 14 |
| Cothi, Afon | 16, 38, 40 | Pembrey | 74 |
| Dinas | 56 | Pembrokeshire Coast Path | 80 |
| Dinefwr Castle | 22 | Pencader | 34 |
| Dolaucothi Gold Mine | 40 | Pendine | 82 |
| Drefach | 30, 32 | Pont-Tyweli | 28 |
| Drefelin | 30 | Poor Man's Wood | 18 |
| Dryslwyn Castle | 14 | Pumsaint | 40 |
| Efailwen | 94 | Rhandirmwyn | 54 |
| Felindre | 30, 32 | St Clears | 86 |
| Gorslas | 76 | St Illtyd's Walk | 74 |
| Gwili Railway | 12 | Scott's Bay | 68 |
| Heart of Wales Line, The | 58 | Sir John's Hill | 90 |
| Kidwelly | 64, 66 | Swiss Valley | 70 |
| Kymer's Canal | 66 | Taf, Afon | 88 |
| Landsker Borderlands Trail | 92 | Talley | 52 |
| Laugharne | 88, 90 | Teifi, Afon | 26 |
| Llanboidy | 92 | Trefenty | 86 |
| Llandeilo | 22 | Twm's Cave | 56 |
| Llandovery | 46, 48, 58 | Tywi, Afon | 8, 14, 16, 22, 54, 56, 58 |
| Llandysul | 28 | Wales Coast Path | 68, 72, 80, 86 |
| Llanegwad | 16 | Whitemill | 10 |
| Llanelli | 72 | Whitland | 84 |
| Llangadog | 64 | Y Garn Goch | 44 |